Trophies, tears and line calls.

Paul K. Ainsworth

DEDICATION

I have been very lucky during my children's tennis to meet so many great parents and coaches.

Stuart was my son's first coach and both my children love his enthusiasm and constant positivity.

Faye, Justin and Jason have all given their input and stretched my children in different ways.

Then there are Richard and Steve who have been there for county cups, competitions and coaching.

My two tennis dad friend, Richard and Bruce who have the manuscript and given their advice along the way through our many conversations in France and the UK.

Finally to the three people who have made it all so special.

My children, Jacob and Steffi who have set me on this journey which has given me so pleasure and tears along the way. Every time they step on court whatever the score, I am so proud.

Lastly, my wife Cathy, who has put up with our obsession and always supported us.

CONTENTS

INTRODUCTION

Over the last seven years I have spent hours practicing tennis with my children, taking them to tournaments and watching them compete. I dare not calculate how many miles I have driven or how much I have spent on their sport.

During our adventures I have also had lots of conversations with other parents about their children's tennis and the struggles that they are enduring. I know there have been occasions when I have not done the right thing as I've tried to encourage my children. I have also seen other parents have very difficult times.

In my working life, I have been a Headteacher of a secondary school and writer on educational issues. I have spent hours researching how children learn best, how we can create the best conditions for children in schools to excel and how to improve teaching.

This book has come about because so many parents have asked me for my thoughts and have suggested why don't I write a book, which draws these skills together to help on the tennis journey. So here it is.

This is not the guide to making the next Andy Murray or Johanna Konta, if a blue print for that is ever possible. Instead this book is for all those countless parents who encourage their children at all levels of tennis, whether it is one group lesson a week, playing AEGON team tennis in the summer or being on the competition circuit from grade 5 to grade 2 tournaments.

Trophies, tears and line calls' is a support manual to help you as a parent deal with the stresses and strains of tournament tennis, help your child reach their potential and stay in the sport for life whether as a player, a coach, a parent of tomorrow or maybe, just maybe, even a professional player.

1 WHY SHOULD YOUR CHILD PLAY TENNIS

How many times have you thought?
- Why do I do this?
- Why do I encourage my child to play tennis?

This could be as you watch your child melt down on court as they struggle with the emotion of losing a match. It would be as you spend another hour in the car driving your child from lesson to lesson or competition to competition.

You might be looking at your bank statement and thinking how do I afford tennis? How much better off would I be if I did not have all the costs of lessons, competition fees, equipment or petrol? Suddenly another holiday is a possibility or even a new car.

We all have days when we think these things!

So why do we do it?

Think for a moment.

What makes it all seem worthwhile?

Is it the day when your child finally beats someone who they have always lost to? Is it the occasion when they got to a final and then won? The happiness on their face as they clutched that little bauble in their hands as you drove them home or placed it next to their bed that evening? Maybe it was just the sight of them hitting forehand topspin after topspin, more poetry in motion than a sport? Or perhaps it is that long-term goal… the idea that your child may play professional tennis one day?

1. Take a minute and jot down why are you a tennis parent.
   -
   -
   -
   -

Tennis parent story…

"I literally fell into the sport. I had no long-term views or aspirations. I certainly wasn't Richard Williams who wrote down a plan for his children. In fact, my only experience of playing the game myself was on old worn tarmac courts with their sad, damaged nets during lunchtime at a big comprehensive school. Instead my son aged 5, went along to Saturday morning sessions at a local school. For some reason he liked it and at the local health club we went to, there were tennis coaches. A fortnightly 45minute lesson become an hour, then weekly and suddenly the hours began to mount. Professional sport was never the aim, I just wanted him and then his sister to enjoy playing sport."

Why play the game?

There are lots of reasons why we should encourage young people and adults to play tennis and they are not generally around trophies, ratings or ranking points!

When I think clearly and honestly these are the seven reasons why I think children should play any sport:

- To have fun – This has to be the key reason for children playing any sport; they must enjoy it and have fun. The best coaches never forget this and you will see children in squad sessions, playing all kinds of games with wide smiles on their faces. It can sometimes be hard for us to maintain fun when we play with our children. It is undoubtedly a challenge to keep those smiles.

- To be with friends and meet new ones – Even though tennis is an individual sport, I've always welcomed opportunities for my children to meet a wide range of players and spend time talking to them. They have made friends with children from all over the country and even from different countries along the way. Relationships have also been formed with other adults; coaches, other parents, team managers and competition officials.

- To learn about sport & improve co-ordination – There is the temptation, especially for boys, to spend hours looking at screens, which can hinder their co-ordination development. Tennis gives our children a chance to let off steam and develop 'physical literacy'.

- To work on their fitness – We want our children running around and building their fitness, it will help keep them healthy and full of energy. As a schoolteacher, I see a lot of youngsters who are unfit and overweight, and this can create problems for years to come.

- To do something they are good at – The more a child plays, the better they get which is good for confidence and self-esteem. This view of being good at something can also help motivate a youngster to keep playing.

- To compete – I have deliberately left this reason. I believe that children gain so much from competition. They learn about themselves and others. These are skills, which will help them in later life. However this must not be the 'be all and end all' when playing. Very few children will be sustained and nourished by continual competition.

- To have fun! Yes, I am repeating myself to illustrate its importance and to remind you not to lose sight of this.

1. How do these reasons match up with your own views? Think about a month's tennis:

    *   Do you children have fun as well as compete?
    *   Do they build relationships and fitness?
    *   Are they developing coordination and self-esteem?

2. If your child does not have such a balance, are they getting the most out of their tennis?

If you look at the points above we could probably split them into physical factors and emotional factors. What is interesting is that four of them are emotional: fun, friendship, esteem and competition, whereas only two of them are physical: physical literacy and fitness.

Physical factors

Tennis is a physical sport. We recognise that the good habits a player establishes in their youth will typically stay with them for the rest of their lives. Have you ever wondered, specifically, how tennis helps with health? Here are a number of reasons:

1. Tennis improves fitness and promotes a healthy lifestyle
2. It is a lifetime sport
3. Players who play at least once a week enjoy a better lifestyle
4. Tennis players tend not to overeat or smoke
5. Tennis encourages good movement in different directions
6. Tennis develops aerobic fitness by burning fat, improving cardiovascular fitness and maintaining higher energy levels
7. At the same time, anaerobic fitness is improved through short, intense bursts of activity (during a point) followed by rest, which helps muscles use oxygen efficiently
8. Players build the ability to accelerate whether through sprinting, jumping and lunging quickly
9. Tennis improves one's reaction time, anticipation, and the ability to explode into action
10. You increase your speed through side-to-side, backwards and forward sprints
11. Tennis players have good leg strength and strong muscles from all those starts and stops

12. Good body coordination is developed by moving into position and then adjusting the upper body to hit the ball successfully
13. Court movement and ball-striking skills means players must have control of their large muscle groups (gross motor control)
14. Delicate touch shots like angled volleys, drop shots and lobs develops fine motor control
15. Good agility emerges from rapidly changing direction many times during points
16. All the starts, stops, changes of direction and hitting on the run develop dynamic balance
17. Children develop strength and bone density, and for lifetime players the risk of osteoporosis is reduced
18. Children develop good nutritional habits. During competitions or a long match they learn what foods to eat and how much to drink to retain energy and to recover
19. Hand-eye coordination builds by timing the oncoming ball with the racquet strike
20. Some children become more flexible due to stretching and manoeuvring to return the ball

Emotional Factors

For many parents, the opportunity for developing a child's mental capacity may be just as important as the physical side of the game. This is certainly true once players begin to compete. There is no doubt that tennis matches are a lonely place to be and the ability for children to deal with this, successfully, can have a huge difference on their future lives.

Which of the following factors do you observe and value in your child's sport?

1. Do they have fun?
2. Is it sociable? Are they developing social skills through interaction and communication before a match, while changing sides on the court, and after play?
3. Can they easily find leagues and competitions to play in?
4. Is their concentration and focus being helped?
5. Does tennis give them the opportunity to set objectives and goals?
6. Do matches help them recognise the ups and down of a competitive world?
7. Are they developing a work ethic as they realise improvement arrives through hard work in practice?

8. Are they developing self-discipline from working on skills in practice?

9. Do they see that patience is required when controlling the pace of play in a match?

10. Have they observed that they can get results by minimising mistakes by playing within their ability?

11. Do they realise that it is their responsibility to make accurate calls in a match no matter what their opponent may be doing?

12. Does preparing their kit and equipment before competition teach them the value of preparation?

13. Are they managing to cope with external factors beyond their control such as the wind or the sun?

14. Are they learning tactics to deal with the mental and emotional stress of competition?

15. Have they started to build their own recovery methods after a long point or a tough match?

16. Do they recognise that managing their nutrition and fluid intake affects their performance?

17. Are they beginning to plan and implement strategies and tactics, which will help them, beat certain players?

18. Do they see tennis as an opportunity for solving problems, often based on angles and geometry?

19. Have they started to consider rituals to calm themselves prior to serving or receiving which can be used in other stressful situations?

20. Are they learning the sportsmanship needed to compete fairly with opponents?

21. Are they learning to win graciously and lose with honour? Gloating after a win or making excuses after a loss does not work in tennis or in life.

It is important to remember that just as developing certain shots is a long term project, tennis also gives your child the opportunity for learning these psychological skills over the long term. This is something that will be covered in more detail in later chapters.

Final Word

It is hard, as a parent, to keep your perspective when your child is in the throes of competition. There will be so many feelings going through your head at times of pressure and stress. Yet it can be immensely valuable to look at these 41 points, focus on them, and consider the ones your child is developing. Physical and psychological development can become your motivation for supporting your child's tennis. This is far healthier than the perpetual study of ranking points or ratings.

2 UNDERSTANDING YOUR CHILD'S MOTIVATION

It is very important that parents gain a full understanding of their child's motivation for playing tennis. There are a number of different levels of motivation and some are more helpful than others in helping your child perform at their best. By reading this chapter you will be able to recognise your child's motivation and encourage them to consider more powerful motivations.

There may be hundreds of reasons why a child should play tennis and why a parent should encourage their child to play the sport. We looked at a selection of these in chapter 1. When your child is very young, they often do not think about why they are playing. You take them to the court and hit with them, you take them to lessons and they play in squads. In fact, you take them to matches or tournaments and they go for it and try to do their best.

However, as your child gets older it becomes even more important to understand their motivation. This may be something you start to consider when they move to green ball and the matches become longer and more intense. It may happen later or it may be earlier. At some point your child will look at you and, in their eyes, you can see them asking 'why am I doing this?' Or they may actually ask you the question as you drive to or from a tennis event.

Tennis parent story...

"My son had a tough day at a grade 4 competition. The draw was not kind and on the first day he lost both matches and then there was over an hour's drive home that night with another hour's drive to the competition the next day for the final two matches. As we made our way there, I can remember him saying, 'I don't know why I do this, I don't think I really like tennis'.

We discussed motivation and various reasons for playing tennis and sport in general and I asked him what he thought his motivation was. His reply was, 'I play because it pleases you and when I do well, you're happy. I was silent in the car for a while as I did not know what to say but what I did know was if this truly was his main motivation, it would make competition ever harder as he grew older."

The Motivation Continuum

Your child's motivation will change at different times during their tennis journey and the following line shows the various states of motivation.

Let's go through each of these stages...

No Motivation

There are occasions when all children have no motivation. They just do not want to play tennis. There can be all kinds of reasons for this and your child may think it for five minutes or it could become a permanent state of affairs.

We have all seen it at some time. You may hear a child say, 'I never want to play tennis again' after a particularly upsetting loss or they may just say, 'I hate tennis.'

Often these comments are uttered in the emotion of the moment or because the child just does not have the reasoning skills (at the time) to properly explain how they feel.

As a parent, we need to pay close attention to such statements, avoid debating them at the time but instead try to identify if our child is sliding into a period of 'no motivation'. Then, we need to consider what actions we can take so that it does not become an on-going belief for which the only solution is to give up the game.

Low Motivation

Tennis players will often go through periods of low motivation. It may be hard to find the enthusiasm to practice or when practicing to give all their energy to the task. If they are playing in a match, it may be that they are going through the motions. They have reached the point when they are not actually bothered whether they win or lose; all they want is for the match to finish as quickly as possible.

Sometime this can occur because they have played too much tennis or they have had a series of losses. As a parent, we have to make sure that our actions do not push our child towards no motivation. Getting cross with someone in this mind-set is not going to help him or her out of it. Instead, it is likely to decrease their motivation further! Yet it is obviously very frustrating if we have driven our child a long way to a match and they appear not to be trying. Or we have paid a lot of money for a lesson to see our child going through the motions or spending more time talking than playing.

Fear of losing

You will see a 'fear of losing' in matches rather than practices and whilst it is higher up the motivation scale than, say, low motivation, such a state will not help the player improve their game.

Losing is not my enemy... fear of losing is my enemy.
Rafael Nadal

We often see a fear of losing in children at key points in a match, such as at game points, set points or match points. The player does not want to risk losing the point and will begin to play very safely by taking power and spin off the ball and hitting the ball towards the centre of the court, appearing to aim at the T. For players who are more skilled they may 'moon ball' which is hitting the ball higher into the air.

It is not uncommon in junior tennis to see both players adopting these strategies such is their desire not to lose the match and rallies can become longer and longer with neither player taking a risk.

There is nothing necessarily wrong in occasionally doing this, nor is there in having a more defensive style of play. The difficulty is that a player does not develop a wide range of shots. In addition, it is likely that a patient better player will generally win. Finally, the player that moonballs is unlikely to make the most of the capability, instead they will always play within themselves.

The need to win

A more positive level of motivation is the need to win. All children want to win matches but there is no doubt that some are more motivated by this than others. The positive side of this can see the player working harder and for longer in a match. They may also be more prepared to go for winners than somebody whose motivation is the fear of losing.

All their talk about tennis before and after matches will be about winning. Which players they can beat and which matches and competitions they can win. 'Winning' will be discussed in more detail in the next chapter.

Desire to improve one's game

The purest and most positive form of motivation for a child to have is the desire to improve their game. It may be a specific shot that they are working on such as hitting a kick serve, a forehand volley or a backhand slice. It is the desire to improve that keeps children practicing and hitting that shot over and over again.

As parents, our aim should be to encourage our children to move to this type of motivation and praise them when they show signs of it. We need to be careful not to place an undue emphasis on match results (wins and losses) or the pursuit of ranking points and ratings. Instead we should be looking to praise our children for their effort and their desire to improve.

1. Take a minute and jot down where you think your child's current motivation is?

   •

   •

   •

2. Why do you think this is?

How do you identify your child's motivation?

Your child may be able to explain their tennis motivation clearly. The parent at the start of this chapter identified their child's motivation by just asking them. However, not all children will be able to explain what drives them, they will just say tennis is something they do. As Andy Murray's twitter biography says, "I play tennis". In addition, and most importantly, children's motivation can and will change and it is our reaction to this, which can solidify the change or alter it. This may not always be in a good way!

Listening and watching your children as they play matches, and also before and after matches, will give you important clues as to their current motivation.

The following table identifies phrases and statements that your child may say on different occasions. You can then use this to work out where they currently are on the motivation continuum.

	Low / No motivation	Fear of losing	Need to win	Desire to improve
Before / after matches	I hate tennis	I hate losing	I love winning	I want to get better
Before / after matches	I'm rubbish	I'm getting worse	I want to win more	I want to get better
Before a match	Do I have to play them?	I can't lose to them	I can beat them	In this match I'm going to…
During a match	I don't care	Don't lose this point… this game	Win this point… win this game	How can I win this point?
During a match	Just hit it	Don't hit in the net	Hit it over the net	In with spin
After a match	I always lose, I never win	I shouldn't have lost	I should have won	I did… really well
After a match	My forehand is rubbish	I keep hitting my forehand in the net	My forehand is great… Did you see that forehand winner	I want to increase the topspin on my forehand.

1. Watch your child prepare for a match, play a match and after a match.
2. What phrases do they usually use?
   -
   -
   -
3. What do you think is your child's current motivation?

What actions can you take?

Our aim as a parent should be to try and move our child's motivation towards the desire to improve their game. If our child is motivated to avoid losing, without the right intervention they may slip towards having low motivation. Again, the wrong action from us can move our child towards no motivation and giving up the game.

Needing to win – Actions you can take:
- Carefully manage competition entries so that your child enters a range of grades of competitions with chances for them to win.
- Discuss goals so that your child has different ways of 'winning'.
- Think about how you praise your child; focus on performance and effort rather than winning.
- Consider rewarding your child for working towards goals rather than winning competitions.

Fear of losing – Actions you can take:
- Try and reduce the pressure on your child, avoid discussions about winning and losing matches but instead focus on performance and effort.
- Encourage your child to play in competitions where they are not expected to win, so a good performance could be a placing in the competition.
- Look for opportunities to play in team tennis, such as AEGON leagues or other winter leagues.
- Could they play doubles; preferable with a child who does not have an intense view on winning or losing.

Low motivation / No motivation – Actions you can take:
- Reduce tennis so that they look forward to playing.
- Increase squad sessions, maybe with players of different ages (younger / older)
- Look for fun tennis opportunities; could they go to adult social tennis sessions?
- Could they play touch tennis or beach tennis?
- Be a hitting partner for a younger child or help with squads.
- Have a break!

- If nothing is working, do not battle; maybe your child needs to try a different sport or activity, which makes them happier.

Final word

A change in your child's motivation does not mean that you are at fault. Children develop their own personalities and as they get older we cannot force them into things even if we think it is in their best interests. What we have to do is try to reduce the pressure on our child, widen their opportunities and look to praise their efforts and their performance… not whether they win or lose.

3 WINNING

We all want to win! As parents, perhaps we want our children to win even more. None of us wish to see our children upset after losing. We know if our child wins they will be so happy and we all want our children to be happy.

However, as much as we want our children to win, we must realise that *we* are the adults and should recognise that the sole pursuit of victory can be unhealthy. We need to ensure that we do not put pressure on our children to win but instead support our children so that they develop and do their best.

This chapter will examine what winning actually means, and how we can reduce the pressure on our children so that they can make better progress.

What is winning?

If your sole focus as a parent is on your child winning every match, then tennis may not be the right sport for you or your child. Remember, in any tournament, only one player wins all their matches. In a weekend junior tennis competition with sixteen players, only one of them will win all their matches, which is six per cent of them.

As a tennis player, you have to get used to losing every week. Unless you win the tournament, you always go home as a loser. But you have to take the positive out of a defeat and go back to work. Improve to fail better.
Stanislas Wawrinka

In a team sport like football or cricket, it is unlikely at the start of the season that we would expect our child's team to win all their matches. We would expect them to win some but recognise they would also lose or draw some of them. To expect our children to enter a tennis competition and win all their matches leads to overwhelming pressure on our youngsters, which can have a negative effect on them.

The negative side of winning

If there is a consistent focus on winning, children can develop bad habits. One of the most obvious of these is cheating. There are lots of opportunities to cheat in tennis. The most obvious are bad line calls. In the vast majority of matches, players are responsible for making their own line calls and it can be so tempting to call a ball out when it is close to the line - especially on a key point. It does not take many competitions to identify the players who are inclined to make 'bad line calls' and it is no surprise that neither the player nor the parent is very popular. We must always encourage our children to make fair calls and that means praising them for their honesty on key points especially if this results in them losing the match.

In addition to poor calls, is the child that repeatedly challenges their opponents' calls every time the ball lands close to the line. The referee is constantly called onto the court and the atmosphere can become very unsavoury. The player is intimidating the other. There is nothing wrong with being assertive but as parents we must highlight the fine line between assertiveness and what is, in effect, an attempt to bully their opponent.

Finally, there is the player that will turn round the score, by not adding a point on or by taking one off. Yes, all children make mistakes but again, but there are some children who do this too often for it to be a mistake. As parents, we are often aware of the score in the match too and if we know our child has made a mistake, the best example we can set is to communicate this to our child.

We want our children to be respected for the tennis they play and not have the reputation of being unfair.

'Beating players we are supposed to!'

Junior players quickly become aware of the tennis rating and ranking system and use this to decide which players they are supposed to beat. As parents, we can also get wrapped up in this and look at competition entries, study draws, and plan a route through the competition. It is easy to then say to our children, 'Oh yes, you'll beat them.' This can increase their confidence but if the match goes the other way, your child either feels that they have let you down or become cross that you have not told them the truth.

Yes, tell your child the ranking of their opponent, because if you don't they will probably read it on the draw, but also discuss with your child that whatever ranking an opponent has, it all depends on how they play on the day. Their opponent may have a really good day or a really bad day. An 8.2 could play like a 6.2 or even a 10.2. Mould the conversation around what your child wants to work on in the match or what improvement they are looking for.

Winning versus improving

There can be a fine balance between winning and improving. Some players will become so focussed on winning matches that they do not think about improving their game. They find a method, which works for them, and stick to it. However, certainly in mini tennis when the ball and court size changes, a method that works in one age range will not necessarily prove as effective in a different age range. So, for instance, in orange ball tennis (under 9s), a player can have considerable success with a game that constantly gets the ball back in. They may not develop a backhand topspin but are prepared to come into the net and stay on the 'T'. In the larger green ball and full ball court, a coach will say that a player needs more weapons and be more prepared to try and win the point. Players need to practise these skills in the younger environment if they wish their success to continue.

Tennis parent story...

I can really remember the pain of my son moving from serving with a forehand grip to using a chopper grip. He spent hours practicing a 'kick serve' and getting more and more frustrated. In competitions, he would serve double fault after double fault and lose matches that he 'should have won'. It was so tempting to say, just serve forehand grip and get the ball in, but I knew he needed to stay committed to the longer-term perspective of having a good serve. Fortunately, his coaches recognised this and continued to encourage him and we got there in the end. He doesn't use a kick serve but he does serve with a chopper grip.

So, if you are not looking at the number of matches that are won, you may think what should your youngster study. Here are three possible ideas to think about.

Improving your scores

It can sometimes be dispiriting for your child to start a match against a child they have never beaten before and are actually unlikely to. We must try to look for the positives in the performance. The most obvious is to highlight any improvement in scores from one match to the next.

When my daughter was playing orange ball tennis, she had two tough regional competitions one after the other, and only won one match over both of them. However, I highlighted that her scores were improving, so for instance there was one player who she lost to 5-7, 1-7 but the next time she played her it was 7-5, 4-7, 4-7; an obvious step forwards.

It is important to choose the right time to discuss this with your child. If they are distraught at losing, they will not take in much of what you say and it is worth waiting until they are ready to listen.

Improving shots

A second element of winning is if your child is improving their shots. On something like the serve, you could look at this statistically and count the number of first serves that go in (and the number of double faults) and see if the numbers improve. You could count any type of shot, but what we often end up counting is the number of errors our child makes. You may choose to look at a different type of shot rather than the serve but be careful not to focus on the number of errors made as this can turn into a negative conversation.

An alternative is to make a note of the shots that you saw which you were particularly impressed with. Such as, 'in the fourth game, you hit some amazing volleys, there was one forehand volley which was great'. If this type of comment starts a positive conversation with your child, this is even better. We will look at both of these ideas again in chapter 12 when we consider performance analysis.

Managing emotions

If your child gets very emotional and shows obvious frustration during a match - you could praise them for not showing frustration too early, such as 'well done for keeping calm all the way through the first set'. You could count the number of positive comments or signs of encouragement they give themselves. Again, any improvements will count as a win. The wins that can mean the most are those ones were your child retains their mental strength and just keeps battling.

> 'That's when you grit your teeth and hang in there and try and find a way to win when you're not playing your best tennis – that's what I can be proud of'
> Lleyton Hewitt

We will look at how you can help your child manage their emotions in more detail in chapter nine.

Final Word

Watching your child win a tight match is a special moment and seeing them win a competition is even better. However, we must try to ensure that winning does not take over. Instead, we need to consider how our child is improving rather than contribute to the pressure of winning.

4 GOAL SETTING WITH YOUR CHILD

Many of our children will practice setting goals in schools. It is very common in both primary and secondary school for children to sit down with their teacher at some point in the year to look at their strengths and weaknesses. The teacher will then work with your child to make some goals, which they work on for the remainder of that school year or for the next year.

You may also find that your child's tennis coach is working on the same technique with your child. This chapter will help you understand the process so you can support progress towards their goal. If coach is not working on goal setting then you can use this chapter to give you some ideas to discuss with your child.

'Everything is possible in life…'
Marat Saffin

Where to start?

Many mini tennis players will have the goal of winning a grand slam, playing at Wimbledon or becoming a professional player. These are obviously very long-term goals and the chance of meeting this goal is very slim. There is nothing wrong with a child writing down this as their dream, ambition or goal but it is unlikely to be the type of goal that you should choose to work on with your child. So don't get too excited about such a goal. Instead you are trying to teach your child goal setting strategies, which will help in their tennis but will also help in other aspects of their life.

> *'I remember as a kid, I was improvising and making little trophies out of different materials and going in front of the mirror, lifting the trophy and saying, 'Nole was the champion!"*
> *Novak Djokovic*

If the right goals are chosen then your child can gain a sense of accomplishment, which can be so important in a sport like tennis, when winning competition can be so challenging. Appropriate goals can foster a can-do attitude as your child works towards them one step at a time.

Tennis parent story…

I can vividly remember reading a newspaper story about Frank Bruno the day before he first fought for the World Heavyweight title in 1986 against Tim Witherspoon, which ended in defeat in round 11. The story explained that as a teenager, Frank has written above the kitchen door, "Frank Bruno, World Heavyweight champion. It took three further attempts for him to win the world title against Oliver McCall in 1995.

As I grew older, I encountered a famous story about a group of Harvard graduates. The most successful were not the wealthiest as children, nor were they the most attractive nor did they achieve the highest class of degree, but instead the most successful were those who had written down their goals as students.

These two stories show the value of goal setting and you could share them with your child or you may have stories of your own.

Explaining goal setting

Your child probably has some experience of saving up some pocket money for a treat such as a new video game or an item of clothing. You can talk about how it takes time and you have to keep putting some money away or you will never be able to afford. You can discuss their feeling at the end when they are able to buy the game or the new top.

Goal setting in tennis

Then link this to tennis perhaps by talking about a certain shot. Perhaps your child is working on serving with a chopper grip or is now trying to develop a kick serve. Just as with money and trying to save a little bit every week. You need to spend some time on practicing the serve each week. It is important to start small so with something that they can achieve. So for instance you would not have the goal of developing spin serves if your child has not begun to learn how to serve with a chopper grip.

How is your child progressing?

Most children will need a method of being able to judge how they are progressing toward their goal. In buying the video game, you may have money in a jar, which is physical reminder to your child that they are getting somewhere. So in serving, at the end of each session could your child practice ten serves and you count how many go in.

Powerful goals

The best goals for your child to work towards are those that they choose themselves. Hopefully this will be something that your coach is discussing with your child too, and they are guiding your child as to the right goal to set. You may have some input by discussing with your child's coach, things that you have observed during tournament play, which would help your child. Between coach and you, your child should then receive a menu of options of areas, which they could set a goal about.

If you can give your child opportunities to practice setting goals in other areas of their lives which you can then support them with, this will give your child valuable experience. The sooner you can start this the better.

Let your child choose their goals

You also need to stay alert to the possibilities of goal setting whilst you are with your child. So if your child plays a match and then says they really want to work on an aspect of their game, perhaps because it didn't go well or the other player was strong in that area, try and record the comment. Even better ask your child to write it down.

You need to take care though that your child does not want to try and achieve something too big too soon. So if they play a big serving child, they are not going to develop a big serve themselves in a few weeks, this could take months or years. If you are not a tennis player yourself, this is were a coach is so invaluable, in that they will be able to break down the goal into more manageable sections which your child can then practice on.

Again the savings example could be used. However often have you heard children starting to save money for big items, perhaps they receive £1 a week and the start saving for an item, which costs £200. Is it any wonder that in this situation, children do not learn saving habits because they can never get there?

You could discuss with your child that it is easier to work towards saving the money for a new video game rather than a new console and use this as a link to their tennis goal setting.

1. Talk to your child about their current goal.
2. Share this with your child's coach.
3. If you both agree it is suitable, ask your child to write down on a piece of card, which they can keep in their bag.

Praise and motivation

You need to keep motivating your child as they work towards their goals. Do not expect the goal to be a motivation on its own, instead, keep encouraging. Praise them by saying how impressed you with how hard that they are working. Give them rewards along the away, these are best if they are effort rewards or for the time they are putting in, rather than their performance. One of the most powerful words you can use is, 'yet'.' You've not got your kick serve, yet!' We will look at this in more detail when we consider 'mindsets' in chapter 11.

Final Word

The skill of goal setting is one, which can stay with your child if they learn it well. It is not something that children can automatically do and children by their very nature are far less patience than adults. So they require lots of encouragement and praise along the way. If you can model good goal setting behaviour this will help, so talk to your children about a goal you are working towards.

5 THE POWER OF PRACTICE

It is the willingness to engage in hard or, quite often, very boring, practice
that distinguishes the very best.

Most people believe that practice is a key component in the success of sportsmen and women. Yet people also think that the very best have an inbuilt gift, which cannot be created. You may have heard people say that it was inherited or that it was 'God-given' and although you can get better with practice – it won't make anyone a world-beater.

People have started to change their minds on this theory, however, and in tennis perhaps a good example of the 'power of practice' versus having a 'gift' are John McEnroe and Ivan Lendl. They both played tennis in the 80s alongside other greats such as Bjorn Borg and Jimmy Connors; a group of players with a rivalry that would compare with Federer, Djokovic, Nadal and Murray of today.

If you look at YouTube videos of John McEnroe, ignore the temper tantrums and you will see rallies and shot making which are simply phenomenal – they led to him winning seven grand slams at a very competitive time in men's tennis. The apparent genius of his play, some would consider to be natural talent.

We can compare this to Ivan Lendl. He went from being a player who was not the best in his country as a youth to being the world number 1. How did he achieve this? Apparently this was through an insatiable work ethic. If we consider the power of practice, Ivan Lendl won eight grand slams, one more than McEnroe.

I made it look so easy on court all those years. No one realised how hard I had to work. No one realised how much I had to put into it. They underestimated my intensity.
Pete Sampras

There are some excellent books available, which consider nature versus nurture in far more detail and which aim to turn the talent myth upside down. These include 'Outliers' by Malcolm Gladwell, 'Talent is overrated' by Geoff Colvin or my own favourite 'Bounce' by Matthew Syed. They do this by highlighting the stories of people we may see as naturally gifted – individuals such as Tiger Woods or Mozart – and explain how they achieved so much at an early age due to the incredible number of hours that they spent on their practice. They also discuss the type of practice and explain how practice is not repetition for repetition's sake but how it is 'highly purposeful'.

In this chapter, we will summarise the ideas from these books and relate them to your child's tennis journey.

What is purposeful practice?

A child who spends a lot of time on court will undoubtedly improve. However to reap the maximum benefit of this effort, they must be engaged in what experts describe as 'purposeful practice'.

Purposeful practice is very specific practice, when every moment is part of the learning experience. The first element of this is that the player is constantly concentrating on what they are doing and gaining feedback on how they can improve. With children the feedback may be from their coach. Skilled coaches will give feedback via questions; how did that shot feel? Why do you think the ball went there?

The second element of purposeful practice is that it is about striving for something that is just beyond reach of the player. If the skill or shot is too difficult then the player will not be able to absorb the feedback. Returning to our kick serve example, this will be a poor choice of practice if they are struggling with the ball toss. There will be too many variables or aspects of the shot that could go wrong and hence the feedback they receive is too much to act upon. Equally the skill or shot should not to be easy. However remember that the simplest shot needs continual practice so to make it more challenging a coach may demand greater accuracy or feed the ball in trickier ways.

Purposeful practice in lessons

When a child is first learning a new skill, or a new shot, they must simply perform lots of repetition. When a child hits one shot and then waits too long before the next one, their body doesn't create enough feedback to feel what is right or wrong. If the shot goes long or in the net, they must simply hit another one and then another one and so on and not be paralysed by an error. You will see many coaches working on this with a child by tossing the ball to the player so the ball lands in a similar place each time and they can groove the shot.

You may have heard of the story of Thomas Edison who after many years of painstaking work invented the light bulb. He certainly did not get it right first time and this is captured in one of his most famous quotations.

'I haven't failed, I've just found 10,000 ways that haven't worked.'
Thomas Edison.

A more recent example of this continual effort can be found in James Dyson's attempt to perfect the cyclone for his vacuum cleaner. He continually kept iterating the shape and design of the cyclone in his workshop until he found the design that was most effective.

Both of these stories illustrate the concept of grooving a shot and using feedback to improve the outcome.

A good coach is often vital in ensuring your child receives the best feedback. They will be able to explain or ask the right questions so that your child understands why something is not working. It could be grip, body position or the shape of the shop. If you do not have a background in tennis, you may struggle with providing this very specific feedback. If you have a very receptive child you may be able to use questions as a source of feedback as we have mentioned above. You could ask your child questions like:

- How did that feel?
- Where did the racquet start?
- Where did it end?
- Where was the ball when you hit it?

The final aspect of purposeful practice is the child being in the right mood to act upon the feedback and want to do more. A child may be too tired physically or emotionally to really engage with the practice. At such a moment a good coach will change or stop the drill, and move the practice on as little value is being gained.

Tennis parent story…

I can remember watching my child at a lesson, he was going through that stage when he did not want to be there and wasn't fully motivated. Instead, he'd hit for ten minutes and then want to sit down. I was getting more and more cross that I was paying for the time he was sitting down and not playing. The coach was using all his skills to cajole and encourage my son to gain value from the lesson. I needed to recognise that the lesson was my son's time and the more pressure I put on him the more counter-productive it would be. Telling him how much money was being 'wasted' would just lead him to say, 'don't pay' Instead, it was the quality of the hitting that mattered and the relationship and trust they were building.

How much should my child practice?

You probably spend a considerable amount of time watching your children play sport and in particular tennis. It can feel like all your spare time is either at the tennis club or at a competition and you probably spend considerable amounts of money for the privilege. So it is no wonder that some parents closely observe this practice. In chapter 16 when we consider 'looking after yourself', one suggestion is that watching your child's practice is not the healthiest thing for you as a parent. One of your key questions is likely to be how much should my child practice?

A central theme of this book is supporting your child so that tennis can become a life long activity and not one in which they are burnt out with by the time they are in their teens. Many parents find it difficult trying to decide how much practice they should offer their child. So let's consider how much purposeful practice it takes, to become an expert tennis player? We can then consider if the amount of practice our child is undertaking is perhaps too much; particularly if our aim is that they become a good player rather than having dreams of professional tennis.

What is '10,000 Hours of Practice'?

Many people will talk about the concept of '10,000 hours practice'. This is the idea that the very best in any field will have completed 10,000 hours of practice. One interesting discussion is does 10,000 hours of practice have to be done so an expert is at their peak, or is this the amount of practice that has to be completed to get them on the starting grid. In tennis terms is the amount of practice required before the player turns professional. It has become one of those ideas that has moved from the realm of research into every day sports conversation.

10,000 Hours of Practice: The Theory

There has been a huge amount of research conducted on how much practice is required to reach the very highest level in any field. In 1993, the psychologist Anders Ericsson was the lead author of a paper, which studied which violinists became the best in their field. They conducted their research at the Music Academy of Berlin, which has an international renown for producing musicians who graduate to play in some of the world's leading symphony orchestra.

Professors at the Academy were asked to group their students into those who had the potential to be international soloists, those who had the potential to play professionally and a third group who would not reach these standards. The researchers conducted a huge range of measures on the three groups. There were many aspects that were the same for all three groups. One example was that the majority of all the students started playing at age 8 and decided to become musicians around 15.

However the key difference was the amount of individual practice the students did. The top two groups were completing on average twenty-four hours a week, whilst the third group did on average nine hours a week solo practice. The researchers then looked at the top two groups in more detail and tried to construct detailed diaries of their earlier practice. They found that by the age of 18 the top group had already accumulated over 7,000 hours of practice. This was before they attended the music academy whereas the second group had totalled over 5,000 hours of practice.

There were other researchers who looked at different fields of expertise. Herbert Simon and William Chase studied chess players and in their findings they proposed the ten-year rule that said no one reached the highest level of chess without ten years of intensive study.

Why 10,000 hours and ten years? This is the idea that it takes ten year to accumulate the 10,000 hours of practice. There are people who seem who have to have achieved mastery at a very young age such as Tiger Woods, Bobby Fischer or Mozart. Tiger Woods won his major golf tournament at 21. Bobby Fischer became Chess Grand Master at 15. Mozart wrote his first symphony at the age of 8. However when experts have studied early lives they all appear to have completed phenomenal amounts of practice by a very young age.

3s

Applying 10,000 hours of practice

We started this section by asking how much should our children being playing and practicing? So if our aim is that our child becomes a professional tennis player, we could work back from the figure that is most often quoted when discussing expertise in a discipline – 10,000 hours of purposeful practice - is required to be a world-class performer.

So what age should we count back from? In recent years the average of the men's top 10 has increased. In 1992 it was 23.2 years, in 2002, it was 24.5 years and in 2015 it was 28.6 years. In terms of the top 100, in 2015 on the men's ATP tour the average age was 27.7 and one the women's WTA tour the average age was 25.5 years.

If we think of a player reaching the highest level by the age of 25 after they started playing at five, this gives us a total of 20 years (it makes the sums easier), to attain 10,000 hours of practice. This gives us a yearly total is 500 hours (or under 10 hours practice a week).

Perhaps from 15 to 25, a player trains full time, perhaps 20 hours week. This actually gives 10,000 in itself. This would seem to indicate that a huge number of hours of training are not required for younger players.

> *If you don't practice, you don't deserve to win.*
> *Andre Agassi*

You may still say that players turn professional much earlier than 25. In tennis many aspiring professionals may seek to gain US college tennis scholarships and aim to go on the tour after graduation. So lets look at achieving world-class performance by graduation or the age of 22? Using the same basis of training full time from age 15, 7 years of training at 20 hours a week. This gives approximately 1000 hours a year or 7000 hours in total. A player starting playing at age 5, then has 10 years to complete the other 3000 hours of practice which gives 300 hours a year or approximately 6 hours a week. We'd expect younger players to train less and the training to increase, as they get older. Again this suggests that children in primary school do not need to be training for countless hours a week.

There are two things that we need to think carefully about. Firstly we are talking about 10,000 hours of 'purposeful practice', the very specific type of practice we described earlier. Secondly this is not saying that 10,000 of practice gives some inevitability of becoming an expert. I am trying to suggest that we should not pressure young people to complete endless of hours of practice at too young an age. Hopefully this puts into perspective how many hours the very best have done and how this number of hours of purposeful practice can be gained over a child's life.

What do the experts say?

Advice from the International Tennis Federation looks at the age of players and places them in certain bands to give a quantity of practice a week. Within their guidelines they suggest that players should be completing a variety of physical activity and not just limiting themselves purely to tennis.

The following table shows these amounts:

Age	Number of Sessions a week	Duration of Session	Total time a week	Activities
6-8	3-4	Maximum 45minutes	3 hours	50% tennis 50% other sports
9-11	3-4	1 hour	4 hours	70% tennis 30% other sports
12-14	4-5	2 – 3 hours	10 hours	85% tennis 15% other sports
15-16	4-5	3-4 hours	15 hours	Tennis / Associated strength and fitness

One rule of thumb that I have often heard said by coaches across a range of sports is that primary age children should train for no more hours in the week than half their age in years. So a ten year old should, do no more than 5 hours training a week and this should be a combination of tennis and other sports, perhaps 4 hours tennis and 1 hour other sport. This is similar to the advice given by the International Tennis Federation.

Tennis parent story…

I can remember when one of my son's regular opponents began attending a performance centre a couple of afternoon's a week. Even though we lived near the same city, the centre was a 40minute drive for them but an 80minute drive for me. There was no way I could get my son there and I felt I was letting him down. It seemed that tennis practice was the like an arms race between super powers as soon as you did one thing, another parent trumped you and got the lead.

I did find my own solution and began to take my son to his regular coach one afternoon a week during the school day. We got more time for the same amount of money and he really valued this time.

The more tennis I watch, I now recognize that comparing your child's practice time is not helpful. You can only do what is right for your child and your family, not get into a race that someone else will always appear to win at the time. What you do not know is the effectiveness of these efforts in the future.

Quality Practice

The two most important elements of practice, which you should look at, are:

- Your child's wish or desire to practice
- How they perform during practice

Children who practice a lot may not view their next lesson as a huge treat, however much money you are spending or the effort you are making. That is entirely normal. Equally if your child is saying they do not want to practice with their coach, you need to think carefully about their current schedule.

It is also important to consider how your child feels when they come off court. The ideal scenario is that after a good practice session not only is the child physically tired but they are mentally tired as well. I have seen coaches particularly in team sport were the early intensity of a practice physically exhausts a child but they are not mentally tired. Think about children on rugby or football pitch spending 20minutes sprinting shuttle runs before they even have a ball to play with. The second is when the child becomes bored often a signal of mental tiredness. An inexperienced coach (this could include us a parent) can easily spend too long on the same drill, which mentally tires the child. Both of these scenarios will stop the practice being purposeful.

Balancing these aspects takes a highly skilled coach. We are looking for quality over quantity. If you are working with your child on their forehand topspin, we want them to hit it enough times so that they are grooving the right shape of shot and imprinting good muscle memory. If we insist of them hitting it too many times so that they are tired, they will begin to replicate a bad shot and imprint the wrong muscle memory. We want our children to practice with their mind as well as their body, as the old maxim states they will then achieve as much in an hour and half than they could in a day!

Final Word

You may feel pressured from talking to other parents that your child needs to practice more. We must try to avoid over practicing which can cause your child to fall out of love with the game. All experienced tennis coaches have seen promising players who practiced too much and drifted away from the game in their early teens. Whereas in reality, there are many years for young players to build up the practice time they need, whether they wish to play at county or international level.

6 THE RIGHT COACH AND PRACTICE PARTNER

You may have played tennis at a high level yourself and possess the technical skills to teach your child how to play tennis. Or you may have never picked up a tennis racket. Yet at some stage you will require a coach to work with your child.

> *"Everyone needs a coach. It doesn't matter whether you're a basketball player, a tennis player, a gymnast or a bridge player."*
> *Bill Gates*

Most junior players will have a coach at some point but it also important that they hit with a range of different people alongside this. This helps practice stay fresh. You will also find that as your child grows up they will value the input from different people at different stages in their development.

I have really enjoyed reading the books by Steve Biddulph, including 'Raising boys' and 'Raising girls' and would recommend both. In 'Raising boys', Steve Biddulph comments on the different relationship that boys have during their childhood. Broadly speaking up till the age of five, boys will firstly look towards their mums. Between the ages of five to ten they start to look to their Dad (or another significant man) as their role model. Over the age of ten, they seek other male role models to follow and learn from. In the world of junior tennis, their coach could be this important person.

If you have a daughter you may consider it equally important for them to have female role model when they reach the age of ten. It is not always easy to find a female tennis coach. I have tried to ensure that in the holidays, we travel to a tennis club further afield so my daughter gains this input. The book 'Untangled' by Lisa Damour which looks at the development of teenage girls is also well worth reading.

This chapter will give you some advice on what to look for in coach and how to tell if the relationship is working. You will soon find that coaching time is expensive so there is also advice on how you can give your child a range of practice opportunities.

Finding a coach

If you are a member of a tennis club it is likely that there will be a coach who has an agreement to work at the club. For small clubs you may find that the coach works at a number of clubs. At bigger clubs there will be a number of coaches who work at the centre. For many children their initial experience of a coach will be a group or squad session that they attend. You may then have to approach the coach and ask if they would be interested in giving your child an individual lesson. Or you may find that the coach asks you!

At larger clubs there could be a system where certain coaches work with mini tennis players and then they are fed through to different coaches as they develop. Or you may just have to choose which coach to contact from a list at the club.

Choosing a Coach

Most children begin their tennis with group lessons and for many children the most important aspect that this coach can bring is fun. The coach, who walks onto court with a smile, is energetic all through the lesson so that your child leaves with a smile is the one to look for. Children need to want to play, so that they are asking you when their next practice session? This is what you are looking for. The worst situation is seeing children waiting in a line as a coach feeds or rallies with one child and then swaps over. We all know that young children will get bored and find their own entertainment, which may not be constructive.

Once your children have played more tennis, you will start looking for someone to provide individual lessons. It is not always easy choosing the right coach and it can be a considerable investment.

What you require is a coach with a passion for the coaching that you are asking them to do. Some coaches are just not passionate about working with 9 year olds whereas others prefer younger children to the possibly surly world of teenagers. You also need to be in agreement with the coach's methods. Watch different coaches around your club, and think about whether their manner will work with your child. Some children are more serious than others and will wish this to be reflected in their coach.

It is important that a coach has the right personality for your child. You wish to see a rapport develop with your child. The best coaches will quickly build this up and your child will tell you if they do not feel this is in place or if they feel uncomfortable with the coach. Other children will not say this outright but instead you will notice they will be less than enthusiastic about attending lessons.

Coaches will have a range of qualifications. To deliver individual lessons the normal expectation is that a coach has the level 3 qualification. More experienced coaches may have a level 4 qualification and be a senior club coach or a senior performance coach. There are also level 5 qualification; master club coach or master performance coach. You will tend to find that the more qualified a coach is the more expensive they are. As we have said at the beginning of your child's tennis journey the qualification level is not necessarily the most important thing.

Your coach needs to be aware of the current standard of junior tennis. They may develop this by running competitions at a club and see whom your child will be competing against. The better coaches will make the effort to occasionally watch your child play in a competition, this may only happen once or twice a season but a coach needs to do this to understand how your child is performing and what is stopping them progressing.

A coach should also have a long-term view, they will be trying to develop a game over a period of months. Some of the things they work on with your child will not always have an immediate impact. Returning to the serving example, it can take a long time for a child to move to hitting their serve with a forehand grip to using a chopper grip but it will be worth it in the in long run. Yet at the same time, you will wish to see a balance of seeing progress in your child's game.

> *"As long as it works for both of us – it's pretty simple. Providing we both want to do it – that's how long I see it continuing."*
> *Andy Murray on Ivan Lendl*

Finally you may decide at some point to change your child's coach. Some parents are constantly chopping and changing their child's coach, almost every season in their attempt to see rapid improvement. I think that this does not send the right message to your child. I would suggest a trial period when you review the dynamics between your child and their coach but after this time, it is a good idea to try and stick with a coach for decent period of time. It may be over time you wonder if things are not working, in which case, try and have a conversation with your coach about this. The best coaches will sit with a parent at regular intervals and discuss what they are aiming to achieve with the child.

If you have built up a good relationship with a coach over a number of years, it can be an agonising decision to move to a new coach. It is important that this is something that your child wants to do. If both you and your child think a new coach is the right thing to do, you have to bite the bullet and have the conversation. At the end of the day you are spending a lot of money and you need to be happy that the money is well spent.

Practice partners

Once you've found a coach, it is likely that you will need to find other people that your child can hit with. The challenge is how you can give your child more court time without breaking the bank. The following passages give some realistic ideas, which you can hopefully employ.

Hitting with Mum or Dad

Certainly before my son moved up to green ball, I was his main hitting partner. We spent hours working our way through sponge balls and then orange balls. A process I am now working through with my daughter. Interestingly it helped my own game too as I was building my technique alongside my son. With sponge ball and orange ball, I used to lose points on purpose so that the games or sets were close. When he moved up to green ball he was less inclined to practice with me and the same is true with the full ball. I found it harder to throw points without him realising too. Hitting with Mum or Dad is the easiest and cheapest practice to organise but there comes a point when it becomes less effective. Perhaps this mirrors the earlier observation that boys over 10 often need different male role models.

When my son moved up to full ball he just did not want to hit with me at all. It was hard not to feel upset by this as I knew I could still give him something of value but I recognised that forcing him to hit with me would be counter productive. If this happens to you, now is the time to find your own social tennis or find another parent to have a hit with.

Squad Sessions

Squad sessions with another coach have added real value as there is another adult giving advice and acting as a role model. Individual lessons with more than one coach can be confusing for a child but group sessions alleviate this because the input is more generalized. Equally it is cheaper than individual coaching. Many parents often wish that there were more squad sessions. If there are not many children at your club who play, you may think that it would be great if children were brought together from across your county for monthly session. This does happen in some areas either through the county system or because a group of parents have asked a coach if they will run it for them.

Apprentice Coaches

In many clubs there are often teenagers who are competing regularly and looking to earn a bit of extra money and will hit with younger players. Sometimes they are working towards their coaching qualifications. In some clubs this is an important part of the provision and parents will use this as much as if not more than individual lessons with experienced coaches. There is no doubt that the children really look up to this type of person especially if they are competing too and will swap stories of competition grades, surfaces and locations. Finding this person is like gold dust as not every apprentice will be right with every child. Some of this will also be age related. The nineteen year-old young man may be great with a ten year old but a nine year old maybe over awed by them.

Tennis parent story…

I've just spent a lovely hour at the tennis club. I've been sat in the cafe whilst my ten-year-old son has been hitting with a nineteen year old, on his Christmas holidays from an American college tennis scholarship. The student at 6 foot 5 towered over my son but they spent the whole hour working hard, hitting balls, analysing what was happening, discussing match situations and best of all smiling. At the end of the session my son said to me, he wished he could have hit for another hour. They used to hit once a week last year whilst Andy was on his year out and it was great to see that the relationship they had built up was still in place.

Hitting with friends

It sometimes seems that some of the hardest practice to organise is hitting with another child of the same age. The first issue is having someone of the right ability and age, though this may be easier at bigger urban clubs. Then there is the issue of competitiveness; whether they can rally without one or the other continually wanting to compete. This can be really tricky in the small world of tennis when they might be meeting each other in competition the next Saturday.

Then there is finding court time, which fits in with two busy families schedules, not always easy to say the least. Maybe this type of practice just happens organically and you have to grab it when it does. So in the summer we'll go on holiday and one of the boys who lives there is the same age as my son and they will rally together for hours. The real advantage of this arrangement is that they won't be on the competition circuit together and have to compete against each other.

1. Does your child have a range of hitting partners?

2. Who do they enjoy practicing with the most?

3. When did they come off court and say I really enjoyed that hit?

4. Have you met any children at competitions who your child enjoyed practicing with?

Final Word

Acquiring the right range of hitting partners for our children to develop their skills without bankrupting us is another balancing act that as parents we are always aiming to achieve. It is probably true that varying combinations will be required for our children at different ages. We need to be careful not force it but instead see how and what develops over time whilst keeping a watchful eye as to what is working and proving effective.

7 PREPARING FOR MATCH DAY

Do you watch your child fall onto court, shoes unfastened, with items falling out of their bag? You then look across at their opponent already coolly stretching for the match. This is one aspect of match preparation but there is much more to it than this. A match outside on a hot sunny day may require a different preparation than the same match on a cold February day.

'I just tried to concentrate on concentrating'
Martina Navratilova

This chapter will give you a range of strategies that you can discuss with your child, so that they can be ready for the match's first point and are able to cope with different situations that may arise. Equally children who learn these skills will be more able to cope with the transition from primary to secondary school, when they have to carry their possessions from room to room. Stereotypically this is often more challenging for boys than girls.

What equipment do you need?

You will soon get used to watching junior players walk onto court with huge bags, which make them look like they have butterfly wings on their backs. You do not need to go this extent but it is worthwhile collecting together the equipment that your child needs.

The starting point is their clothing. No one knows what the weather will be actually like and often you may not be sure whether your child is playing indoors and outside. So children need a range of clothing such as skins, a sweatshirt and track suit trousers in the case of cold and a cap/visor, sunglasses and a towel in the case of it being hot or sunny or both.

Try to leave this in your child's bag so it is available for practice as well as matches. It is always good to check the equipment the night before and even better is if you can get your child into the habit of doing this. For mini tennis players this is also good practice for secondary school but some children are not necessarily mature enough to do this themselves and you need to take time to build these behaviours.

Timings

Depending on where you live, you may find that the journey to a tennis competition is not a short one. Children do not tend to understand the timings for tennis tournaments or the length of the journey. What you wish to avoid is running out of the car straight onto court for the first match. Equally some children find it quite stressful to sit at the venue for an hour before their first match.

You usually get emailed about the time of the first match, and then check this with how long the journey is and explain this to your child with the time you have to leave. Try and understand how long your child needs to prepare at the venue for their match. Remember all children are different. Over time you will realise which venues have courts available before the competition for practice, and those, which do not.

Meals

One of the difficulties of tennis tournaments is working out when to eat. Children need food to be able to play properly especially when the matches become longer and longer and they have a number of them on one day. You need to decide if it is better to have an early meal before setting of? Or do you plan to eat in the car on the way to the venue.

You also need to ensure that you have a range of food and drinks with you to keep your child strong over the day. Not just snacks but sandwiches too. Most children drink energy drinks when they are playing and they will soon learn that they need to alternate sips of those with water or they may get indigestion.

"Tennis is mostly mental. Of course, you must have a lot of physical skill, but you can't play tennis well and not be a good thinker. You win or lose the match before you even go out there."
Venus Williams

Leaving the house

The flash point is often leaving the house. You may start getting anxious yourself about the tournament, as might your child. You get cross because you think you are running late and suddenly start firing questions about whether they have the right equipment for the day. So try, try, try to get organised and check this the night before.

1. Is your child organised the night before a competition?

2. How could you help them with this skill?

3. Do you get stressed leaving the house for competitions?

4. What could you do to make this easier?

Looking at the draw

At many tournaments the draw is published in advance and if it isn't you will always have a list of the players competing. You will probably see the draw but you need to decide how much you wish to share with your child.

Some children like to see a list of the players competing so they can have a realistic view of what they are playing for. They may want to look at the draw in advance to plan how they may play against different players. Equally some children play better just turning up, seeing who is on the other side of the net and do not like the information in advance.

You may choose to go for a half way house and if your child has a bad draw such as having a player they don't like playing against in the first round or meet the 1st seed early, decide to plead ignorance about the draw. As your child gets older they are likely to want more information and will start to think about what tactics they can employ to beat their opponent. The age this happens varies so much and the only way you will learn is by trial and error. It is worth taking a lesson from the pro's though and not looking to far ahead in the draw, just telling them the first match or who is in their group is probably enough information for them to process.

Tennis parent story…

I can always remember a green ball tournament by son was in and studying the draw with him. He was lacking in confidence but was the number 1 seed. I went through the list of players and pointed out that apart from the number 2 seed, he had a good chance, they were mostly players he had beaten and there were a couple of children who had never played a tournament. In fact I showed him he had a bye in the first round and would play the winner of two such children.

His first match came and whilst the player had never played a competition, he was very, very good. He beat my son and went onto easily win the competition and the following week played in a grade 3 tournament and came 2nd!

My son won the rest of his matches and came 5th, but still said to me afterwards, 'you said I would get to the final of this competition'. Pointing out that he won more games against the eventual winner than any other player did not really help.

Coaching in the car

One of the best pieces of advance I have received is never coach in the car on the way to tournaments. One psychologist wrote that coaching in the car can give your child the subliminal message that you do not believe they are capable. My thought is simpler; our job in the car to ensure our child is relaxed as possible so that they can play their best. So yes give them a brief reminder of a key point that you and their coach have discussed but then try and have a conversation about anything else rather than the specifics of the tournament ahead. Try and avoid having a relentless focus on tennis but instead discuss wider issues. You will have enough time during the tournament to discuss tennis!

Think about the most successful competitions that your child has played in and then reflect on these three questions.

1. What does your child like to do when they arrive at a competition?

2. Do they like to practice with you or other players?

3. Do they like to know who they are playing in advance and talk tactics?

Final Word

Preparing for matches does not happen by accident and you won't always get it right. It is a really useful skill for your child to develop which is transferrable to other aspects of their lives. So try and spend time thinking about how you do this and of course talk to your child about the process too.

8 DEVELOPING MATCH ROUTINES

All players develop their own match routines and you will wish to help your child find positive ones. You will want them to be able to approach and plan out their match so they make the best of their skills. Equally important is that they can replicate often-straightforward shots and techniques under pressure.

At less pressurised moments, such as during practice a certain aspect of a player's game can break down. They may suddenly start double faulting. The player that has routines which they can return to, will often be able to cope with these difficulties more effectively.

This chapter will help you work with your child so that they can develop their own match day routines to make the most of their game.

Pre-match tactics

How often have you watched your child play a match and become increasingly frustrated, that if they could do one thing differently they would have a much better chance of winning the match? The goal is for a child to be able to think through matches, notice what is working and do more of it. If a strategy is not proving effective, they can identify this and change tactics. This is a very sophisticated skill, which takes time to learn and we need to help model it.

In mini tennis, pre match tactics can be very simple. If your child is playing outside, look at the weather conditions and always have the sun or the wind behind you. If you win the toss don't necessarily choose to serve, choose the best end if the weather is an issue. If the other player makes a decision on serve you can still choose an end. If the game is inside or is unlikely to be affected by the weather then most children will ask their opponent to serve first.

Many junior tennis players have a weaker backhand and children quickly learn to hit to this side. We will also see our children continually hit to a left-hander's forehand so engrained are they to hitting to a right-hander's forehand.

You want to encourage your child to look at their opponent during the warm-up rather than trying to win every practice point. Firstly are they left handed, think which side is their backhand. Secondly watch their play, are they particularly weak on one side, is this a side you can attack? How deep do they hit the ball? If they are not strong or are playing into the wind, do not stand so deep.

These are the basics of pre-match tactics but for many children this does not happen automatically, it is something that you will build up over time. You could even have a little card to take on court, which they could look at to remind them. It could just have the following points written down:

- Left hand or right hand?
- Hit to the backhand.
- Am I standing too deep?

You may feel that choosing an end and then thinking about these three points is very simple. It can still take a while of trial and error for a young child to understand; so do not expect them to manage all of this at once. Instead select one of these aspects to focus on and then praise your child when they get it right!

When your child is happy and confident with these aspects of pre-match tactics you can increase the complexity of match routines. For instance have they played the child before, what were the strengths or weaknesses? Common themes here are being inconsistent on one flank in which case they need to aim to this side. Does their opponent slice the ball or play drop shots, in which case they need to be ready to move forwards if they hit the ball to a certain side. Is their first serve or second serve very different in which case, think carefully about where to stand? These ideas can take children a long time to use confidently and consistently, so praise every small step forward, which your child takes.

Plan B

Finally what happens if their plan is not working? What happens if the match is slipping away from them? Is there something different they can do? Could they try and use some drop shots? Can they moon ball and hit the ball deep and high? Could them come into the net and hit some volleys? None of these aspects may work but if your child can start to try something different if things are not going according to plan it can give them something to look for and some positivity when things are against them.

Managing yourself

A very important aspect for junior tennis players to learn, especially boys, is how to manage themselves during a match and a competition. This skill is transferrable to other aspects of their lives. Even at the under ten age bracket, they could play a match which last over an hour and a half and on a hot day if the match is close it may be the child who looks after themselves the best is the winner rather than the child who appears the 'better' tennis player.

> *'Sometimes I wish I could have been a bit more relaxed, but then I wouldn't have been the same player'*
> *Steffi Graf*

The first element of this is making sure your child is properly prepared for the match in advance as discussed in the last chapter. Things like ensuring they have a cap and sunglasses on hot days.

The following checklist builds on this and could be something which you share with your child:

1) Take your time between points
2) Always bounce the ball when you are preparing for your second serve.
3) Whilst preparing to return serve keep bouncing on the balls of your feet ('happy feet')
4) Encourage yourself in between points even if you make an error
5) Keep your sunglasses and baseball cap on,
6) Each game wipe your face with a towel
7) At a changeover <u>always</u> sit down and take a drink.

Each of these have been worded positively as an action to do rather than something not to. There will be other aspects that you wish your child to focus on rather than these seven points, so why not replace them with points you wish your child to work on.

Tennis parent story...

Like most tennis fans, I can remember vividly the day Andy Murray won his first Wimbledon title. I spent that Sunday afternoon in front of the TV watching the Murray / Djokovic Wimbledon final, marvelling at the physical and mental strength of the two players involved in rallies frequently over twenty shots on such a warm day.

Only a few hours earlier I had taken my son to his own tennis competition. It was a scorching morning for ten year olds to play three matches, all best of three short sets.

In his first match he walked onto court with his carefully packed tennis bag containing drinks, sun glasses, baseball cap and in pride of place the new purple hand towel he had bought on his Monday visit to Wimbledon.

He won his first two matches and there is no doubt that he carefully managed himself in the heat.

In the third match, the sun was really beating down on both players, the rallies were long with my son going for his shots whilst his opponent went for less pace and a more defensive game plan, concentrating on keeping the ball in. My son fell behind but I didn't mind as I would rather him get good practice of going for the right shot even if the operation does not always work.

However what was noticeable than as the games went on and the sweat began to pour, the techniques he had used in earlier matches were forgotten; drinks were not taken, points were rushed, the sunglasses and hat removed, the towel ignored and self talk became more negative.

He lost the match and the other boy should be congratulated for sticking with his game plan. I don't mind that he lost, as there is an excellent learning opportunity for him to consider how he manages himself in the future. So during the Murray / Djokovic final we played 'managing yourself' bingo and Andy Murray's use of the towel in between points was one excellent example of this.

1. Why not write a checklist in a notebook, which your child could look at in between games.

2. Keep a tally of all the things your child does.

3. Keep this positive and praise them for the match routines they follow

Visualisation

The art of visualisation is one of the skills of Neuro Linguistic Programming (NLP). Training your mind to visualise a positive event, can help remove negative thoughts and aid you to gain the outcome you are looking for.

'My mental coach taught me very simple things such as creating a system and routine in your daily life that helps you work'
Thomas Berdych

Developing visualisation takes time and patience. We all know when we are working with children especially our own children; time and patience are not always in abundance.

We can help our children develop a performance routine, which is one aspect of visualisation. Probably one of the most memorable performance routines was the one used by Jonny Wilkinson prior to taking a penalty kick. The squat, the cupping of the hands, the looking up at the rugby post, look at the ball, look at the posts, look at the ball and then run and kick the ball. In the world of tennis we can look at Andy Murray always taking three balls or Rafa Nadal's idiosyncrasies prior to serving are almost a performance routine. Whether we want our children to spend a considerable time adjusting their shorts is a debatable point!

Virtually every player has a problem with their serve at some point especially on pressure points and developing a performance routine for the serve is something we can work on with our children. You could even practice it at their bedtime.

The following is such a performance routine:
1) Adjust racquet strings
2) Select a ball
3) Deep breath
4) Approach base line
5) Position feet
6) Chopper grip
7) Look at the ball
8) Look at the target
9) Think of the serve going in
10) Say "Hit through"
11) Toss ball & serve
12) "ACE!"

You could use this performance routine with your child, why not act it out with them and visualise the ball going over the net and in. Perhaps with your own sporting commentary. Then see if over time it helps their serving confidence?

1. Write the service performance routine on a piece of card

2. Place the card in your child's tennis bag

3. Make a second one which they could use as a book mark

Final Word

Helping your child develop match routines can be very rewarding; you will see your child put them into practice until they become automatic. This can take time and needs to be seen as a long-term process. There are a lot of ideas in this chapter, so try to select one of the ideas to work on as children can become confused with too many ideas and as a result the routines can be a hindrance. Always look for opportunities to praise, focus on what they did do rather than what they didn't and hopefully these ideas will increase your child's success.

9 MANAGING EMOTIONS

One of the hardest aspects of tennis and indeed any individual sport for both the player (and in junior sport, the parent) is managing emotion. How often do we watch a tournament and see a child have a tantrum or be distraught beyond reason about a particular loss? How often do we wince at the comment another parent makes to their child? We all need to manage our emotions, both parents and players.

This chapter looks at techniques that you can discuss with your child and also positive strategies that you can use which will provide support for your child in managing their emotions.

Thinking of your child as
behaving badly
disposes you to think
of punishment.

Thinking of your child as
struggling to handle
something difficult
encourages you to help them
through their distress.

Upset during a match

'So there was a fire inside me. And that fire inside you, it can be turned into a negative form or a positive form. And I gradually realised that I had this fire and that it had to be used in a positive way.'
John Newcombe

We have to recognise that if our child is upset during a match there is little we can do to change their manner or mood. In addition if our child is emotional after a match, it is unlikely that the interaction we have with them will quickly solve this. Most of us have probably done this though, child is upset about an aspect of the match and then we get cross with them. If we think about this logically, if our child has become upset and angry due to something that has happened in the game, are we behaving any better in mirroring this ourselves by becoming cross with them?

A parent may tell you of an instance when their child banged their racket or got angry and they told them that if did it again, they wouldn't play again and it miraculously it worked. We can then feel a failure that when we try the same thing, it makes no difference. I have also seen other parents reprimand their child during a match for poor behaviour and it make a little difference, in fact sometimes it can make it even worse.

We have to see managing emotions as a long-term project and most of the work we will do, will not be on the day of competitions but before or after. The most important action we can take during competition is to try and remain calm and model the behaviour that we wish to see from our child.

A crisis of confidence

When children lose control of their emotions, it is often because they feel they have not done as well as they should have. They have lost a point, game, set or match which they believed they should have won. They can feel overwhelmed by the challenge that they have faced or are facing. We can spend huge amounts of angst considering what is the right thing to do? Is it more lessons or fewer lessons? Play in more competitions or fewer competitions? Does the child need more fitness training or less training?

'You've got to take the initiative and play your game. In a decisive set, confidence is the difference.'
Chris Evert

There are occasions when the results do not seem to be going our child's way. One thing we can do is look at our child's intentions. Are they trying to do the right thing but the execution is just not quite accurate enough? Is it a physical factor and they are having a growth spurt or their hormones are affecting them as they mature? In which case we should retain our children's current training programme, providing they are enjoying it. One strategy we may undertake is to reduce the number of competitions or the grade of competition though, until our child is ready.

Our child could be suffering from a crisis of confidence. In their eyes they feel they are having a poor set of results and their confidence is knocked. They feel that everyone is getting better than them and they are getting worse.

Tennis parent story…

My son will say to me that he doesn't feel he is getting better because he cannot see any change especially if the results aren't going his way. Yet I can certainly see he is getting better as I have to work ever harder in our occasional hits to stay competitive with him. Unlike his peers my game is not getting any better!

Coaching confidence is as important as coaching shots

One way of helping build this confidence is to use techniques from life coaching and Neuro-linguistic programming with your child. Life coaching is a form of mentoring, which gives individuals the confidence and ability to move forward in a positive manner areas of their lives where they crave change. Life coaching is an approach that looks at the present and sets goals for successful future. For our children, success could be walking tall onto the court and approaching a match with a can-do attitude. If they can do this they will find managing their emotions becomes more possible.

> *'Older people make this mistake all the time with younger people, treating them as a finished product when in fact they are in process'*
> *Andre Agassi*

In supporting our children deal with their tennis emotions we do not necessarily need to consider the long-term goals which adult life coaching may look at. However the techniques which coaches use to help people work towards their goals are very useful. These tend to be developed from Neuro-Linguistic Programming (NLP), which simply means training the brain to act in a certain way, particularly when under stress.

Four popular techniques are positive diaries, walls of confidence, visualization and affirmations. We have already briefly looked at visualization in the last chapter.

Positive diaries

This technique aims to help your child capture the days when things have gone well with the aim of returning to this mind-set at other times. After your child has played a match or a tournament, ask them this question, what three things have they done well? You need to write these down for your positive diary.

If they have lost and feel they have played terribly, they may find this really difficult and it may be something that you have to return too once they have calmed down. During their matches you may have been recording your own positives so you have some good things to say, no matter what the scoreboard says.

You are looking for very specific points. If they have been working on serves in a lesson and it has gone, well jot this down. You could be more precise and if their 1st serve percentage was high and double fault percentage was low, write this down. At a future event, if the serve has gone badly, you can highlight instances of when it worked well and use this as a positive, 'you can do it'.

Similarly read through the positive diary with your child if they are facing a tough match, either against a much higher rated player or maybe one of those occasions when you just know it's going to be close. If they can go on court thinking of previous positive experiences it can only help them.

Not many of our children's coaches are able to attend competitions so you could encourage your child's coach to spend five minutes discussing the positive diary with your child, so that your child cab explain their positive statements. Hopefully this will mean that they begin the lesson in a good frame of mind too.

Wall of positivity

Building on the idea of the diary is creating a wall of positivity in your child's bedroom. This can be quite a fun task to work on with your child.

If your child has gained trophies from their tennis (or any activity) these are often very treasured possessions of which the value to your child (and to you) is disproportionate to their monetary value. These small items are obvious examples of the positives that your child has gained from their sport. However these medals or trophies will only be a small amount of the success that your child has had and are only some examples of the positives.

Why not make some posters in your child's bedroom (can be as simple as drawing on A4 paper with felt tips pens). You could make lists of your child's competition 1st and 2nds. Some tournaments do not give out 'silverware' and it can be easy to lose track of those good results. If there are few of these, keep track of 3rd and 4th places too.

You could make a second set of posters with your child's ranking at the end of each season (county, regional and national). This has been particularly useful when your child changes age range and is starting from the bottom again. Children often forget this journey and remember the end points along the way and forget the progress they have made.

Thirdly create some signs with your child's name in and pictures of them playing. One could be '—— is a top tennis player' and the second '—— is champion tennis player' with the date of their first competition win.

Fourthly you could make sets of motivational posters. One idea is to develop tennis alliterations with your child. Make a sign saying ' - - hits…' followed by a tennis alliteration. Here is a list of possible phrases to get you started:
- Ferocious forehands
- Slamming serves
- Venomous volleys
- Devilish drop shots
- Blistering Backhands

Self-affirmations

If you listen to children during matches and sometimes even during training you will hear them either criticizing themselves or telling themselves not to do something. Common things heard:
- Don't hit it in the net
- Don't lose this point
- I keep double faulting
- Why do I keep hitting it out?
- I'm so bad!

If you tell yourself not to do something, strangely the more likely it is to happen. So if a player says before a second serve is 'don't hit it in the net', the more likely they are to do it. In addition, the sooner a child begins to talk negatively or criticise themselves in a match, the deeper and darker the emotions become.

One of the most powerful ways of managing emotions is positive self-talk. This is something that many sports people use to raise their performance. It is something that can be learnt and should be practiced. A good way to start this process is to spend some time discussing with your child positive things they can say during play. Some suggestions include:

- I can do this
- One more point
- In with spin
- On my toes

You could make these as posters for your child's room or have them on a cue card for changeover time. I have seen affirmations on wristbands too or the cheapest version, write one on the back of your children's hands for when they are playing.

Visualisation

Older children and teenagers may wish to explore these ideas further and practice visualization. In the chapter eight an example of visualizing the serve was given.

Visualising uses all the senses so that athletes can see themselves performing to the best of their ability. The starting point can be for a player to remember a situation or match when things have gone really well.

They try to take themselves back to the performance and use all their senses to remember or recreate it. The player asks themselves some questions:

- What exactly could you see?
- What were the colours?
- How bright was the light?
- What could you hear?
- What did you feel when you were hitting the ball?
- How were you moving about the court?
- What were your emotions?

The aim is become so immersed in the mental image that it feels as if it is actually happening. The player is imagining performing the activity from their perspective and not from that of the audience.

"I have sat on Centre Court with no one there and thought a bit about the court, the matches I have played there. I want to make sure I feel as good as possible so I have a good tournament."
Andy Murray

This takes practice; it is not wishful thinking or a brief moment. The imagery should be so detailed that it takes almost as long to execute in your mind, as it would take in real life. Some athletes will even write this down, however this should not be a barrier for a child trying visualization.

You could encourage them to think about a match where they have played really well and showed careful control of their emotions. What was different that day? How did they manage to do this? You could also think about a match when they have come back from behind, perhaps they lost the first set 6-0 or 4-0. They might have been saved multiple match points and come back to win. The key is for your child to visualise their successful moments as this will give them confidence when they are facing challenges.

Before a child begins a match, they could practice this visualization to increase their confidence.

1. Which of the following do you think would be most effective with your child?

    - Make a wall of positivity
    - Brain storm tennis alliterations
    - Keep a positive diary
    - Develop a list of self-affirmations
    - Practice visualisation

2. When your child is in right frame of mood, take one and try it with your child?

Final Word

There are no quick and easy answers to help your child manage their emotions. There will be some days when they manage it well and others when they become distressed during the first game of a match. They will seem to make progress and also go backwards. You cannot control your child from the side of the court and if you try to do so, you may increase your child's anxiety / stress and as a result make managing their emotions even harder.

The key is to remain patient and work to build the child's confidence. As a tennis parent those are two maxims for us to keep hold of. All children will have dips at times. We must show the patience that children find so difficult no matter how challenging this is for us. If we cannot achieve this, how can we expect our children to do the same. We must always be looking for opportunities to build their confidence. If our children can learn their own coping strategies for dealing with such misfortunes through their tennis, they will have gained an invaluable skill for the rest of their lives.

10 STEPPING OFF COURT

One of the biggest challenges is to understanding what is the right thing to say to our child when they step off court. Our first words can make a huge difference, positive or negative. Equally what we say on our journey home can also be hugely significant This chapter will makes suggestions as to how you can best motivate your child and deal with their emotions straight after the match.

No words needed

There are occasions when no words are needed, when your child is so disappointed, that the best approach is to give them a hug or to just sit next to them in silence. There is of course a difference between companiable silence and threatening silence and with all such things it is about perception. There needs to be some verbal or non-verbal communication, so that your child recognised that this is not the quiet before the storm but that you share their pain too.

First words

However badly the match has gone, in the aftermath we need to find something positive to say. There must be something that they did well during the match which your can highlight. If you cannot think of anything, then perhaps the best response is just to say how sorry you are. You could be honest and agree that everyone has a bad day at some point. With many children, once they begin to speak, discuss their match or describe their feelings, the sooner that they can process what has happened.

> *'You live during the match and you have strong emotions, but you don't want to get too overexcited. My body's totally flat now. I cannot move anymore. Just because of the tension out there'*
> *Roger Federer*

What we must desperately try not to do is criticise or get angry; as such comments are the soonest way to turn them off the sport. This can be really hard, and is a learning curve for us. We all have occasions when we have been cross with our child for their behaviour on court; normally not about their tennis but for the way they have mishandled their emotions. If we do get cross, then once the emotion has drained away, we may need to apologise to our child.

On particularly disappointing days, pulling into McDonalds on the way home can prove the best strategy. Sometimes an emotional response can be due to being very low in energy as getting upset can be as draining as the physical element of being on court. So getting some food into your child or a big milkshake can be the starting point in being able to discuss what has happened.

Starting the conversation

Often it is a good idea to start conversations with questions to see if we can get our chid talking. One blogger described sets of four words that we should never say to our child:
- How did you do?
- How did it go?
- Did you win today?
- How was your ... (backhand, volleys, kick serve)?

The blogger commented that even with good intentions, if a parent constantly asks their child these questions, they feel that they are being either constantly interrogated or judged on the day's performance. I think this is an interesting concept but more suited to secondary aged youngsters rather than primary aged children.

It is worthwhile thinking what are the most effective pieces of communication that you can give your child. One suggestion after a loss is, 'tell me the positives?' We are all aware that moving a child back onto a positive track is so important when they have a series of matches to play. You can also ask, 'What went well?' Many children will be able to recite in their opinion everything they did badly. So watch and try and remember one great rally to try and remind your child of. 'Do you remember that amazing backhand slice you hit?' What we are trying to do is, begin a positive conversation and get them feeling upbeat about tennis again.

We all realise that with all conversations the trick is timing. If we ask our children these things too soon after a match, they will not be receptive and whatever we say will not help them move forwards.

Tennis parent story…

I can always remember one occasion when my child was playing in a round robin competition and had six matches. On paper he was the number one seed and gone into the competition expecting to win. He lost the first match in a tiebreak and was really upset, not wanting to play again.

I gave my best motivational speech, pointing out all the positives of his game and then gave some hard messages that he had to get back on court and play his matches. I stopped, he looked at me and said with heavy sarcasm, 'Great motivational speech dad' and stomped off to play his match. For a moment my blood boiled and then I just had to laugh. He had certainly pricked my pomposity!

Difficult conversations

There will be occasions when we need to have more challenging conversations with our children. Sometimes our child will honestly ask why they lost and there may have been something very obvious in the way they approached the match either from a technique or mental perspective. It is advisable to not to have this discussion straight after the match, why not leave it till another day or even have this when coach is there who is likely to neutralise the conversation.

If you are having such a conversation do not give lots of negative feedback, keep it to two or three key points and in addition do not labour them and keep going over them but instead include positives too. In my world of education, I have heard this described as a 'poo sandwich'. Start with a positive, and then give the negative before returning to the positive.

If you are disappointed with their behaviour during a match, you do need to challenge them on this but try and avoid it becoming personal; one tactic is to say you are disappointed in their behaviour and not in them. We all have listened to some parents talking about one point and going over and over it. This can be worse if two parents are there and as soon as one parent stops talking, the other starts on the same topic. Try and highlight a time when they did behave well and talk about how they felt differently then.

Praise

So far this chapter has focussed on what to say when things have gone badly as surely it is easy to know what to say when the match has gone well. Recently there has been a lot written about 'Mind-sets' and they way we praise our child can have a big impact in whether they develop a growth mind-set i.e. they have the ability to cope with setback and find strategies to overcome them rather than having a fixed mind-set which is when people of convinced of their own talent but when things go wrong they lose their ability and focus. This will be covered in the next chapter.

1. How have you helped your child best after a difficult loss?

2. How do you start conversations with your child?
   - What works well?
   - What doesn't?

3. How can you avoid conversations and confrontational?

4. How often do you praise your child?

Final Word

'I never look back, I look forward'
Steffi Graf

Having the right conversation can be very challenging. We have to be honest and accept that we will not always get it right. Even if we feel we said the correct thing it may not have the impact we hoped for. So try not to be hard on yourself or your child. Talk to other people about how they manage such conversations. Remember sometimes the best decision is to choose not to start the conversation at all.

11 MINDSETS

There is considerable research into the impact that a child's mindset has on their performance. On a very basic level, we have all seen our child walk onto court in a bad mood and struggle to perform. The American author, Carol Dweck has analysed this area and published her findings in the book 'Mindset: How you can fulfil your potential'. This has been widely used in the UK and the USA. In the world of education it is a set of ideas that have been seized upon by teachers and school leaders to try and help children achieve their potential.

In this chapter I want to help you to apply it you child's tennis and junior sport in general by giving you some suggestions as to how you can encourage your child to get the most out of their practice and more importantly deal with that thin line between triumph and disaster which flows through all sport and is amplified in individual competition.

As with all things that you will work on with your child, this is not a quick process and there will be days when you see your child show a growth mindset and probably more days when they do not. Try not to criticise your child if they seem locked in negativity and do not expect to immediately turn your child's mood round. It just means they haven't solidified their growth mindset, yet! All children struggle at times and we just try to do what we can to support them.

"We like to think of our champions and idols as superheroes who were born different from us. We don't like to think of them as relatively ordinary people who made themselves extraordinary."
— *Carol S. Dweck*

Growth and fixed mindsets

Do you ever wonder what is it that makes some children and young people really want to practice a skill, whether its drawing or a certain tennis shot? When you are looking at your child train or play in a match, what attitude do they display? Do they believe that with practice that they will improve; they will learn certain shots or are they convinced that they are just better than some children and that other children are better than them? If so why do they think these things?

Two years ago I read "Mindset", which shed some light on this. The book really stayed with me. It was also one being read throughout the education world at the time but interestingly has not necessarily become a go to read in the world of sport.

When I read the this book I was providing intensive support to three schools specifically in the final push towards GCSE Maths examinations. I was fascinated by the different approach the students took to their learning. Every student I worked with was positive about their studies; they enjoyed working with me and wanted to gain a good grade. Yet some were prepared to practice and others could not bring themselves to do it irrespective of the grade they were at.

I felt their mindset was making difference. Carol Dweck said there were two mindsets, which I would suggest are on a continuum. At one end is the fixed mindset. These are the students who in their hearts believe that basic qualities are fixed traits, which cannot really be changed. Mathematical skill is something you are born with; it cannot be altered. These children believed that talent was key to a student's success. One group told me about a student who scored 197 out of 200 in their Maths GCSE mock. "He must be well clever' they said and began to discuss what it must be like to be so clever. In tennis terms this is the child who believes they are better than one player but another is better than them. If they lose to the first child they will be beside themselves. Before they go on court with the second they have already lost.

At the other end of the mindset continuum is the growth mindset. This is the belief that all qualities can be improved. Effort and resilience are the keys to success. These are the students who are prepared to put in the high levels of work; these are the students who completed the practice papers. My reply about the maths student was, 'no he's not born really clever, instead he's put loads of effort in, and he's tried really hard.' I can remember the children looked at me curiously and then one of them said, 'yeah he works for 4 hours a night, every night' the conversation moved on as to why they could not do that as they would have no social life.

I suggested that 4 hours were not necessarily required; if they had spend 20minutes a night on Maths since the start of year 10 every one of them would now be on a grade B. A few of the students then said how they wished they could start year 10 again. I asked them about doing 20minures a night from now? Sadly this seed still fell on stony ground, as they did not truly believe that practice would make much difference to their grade. In tennis terms the child with the growth mindset, will believe that they can practice and will improve and will also recognise that another child can improve too.

With our children whether it is in tennis, sport or the academic world, we need to be trying to develop a growth mindset so they believe that there is no limit to performance if you are prepared to practice enough.

Identifying mindsets

You have probably been thinking about whether your child (or even you) displays a fixed or a growth mindset. I believe it is little more complicated than always having one or the other. Firstly there is a continuum between the two, so two people may have a growth mindset but one is more secure in this than the other. Secondly I think someone's mindsets can change in different areas. For example you might say that someone can either draw or they can't, hence a fixed mindset. Yet at the same time you may say that with revision for Maths someone can improve his or her score or grade, hence growth mindset.

Summary of 'Dweck's Mindsets'

Fixed	Growth
Ability is static	**Ability is developed**
Avoids challenge	Embraces challenge
Gives up easily	Persists when faced with obstacles
Sees effort as fruitless	Sees effort as necessary
Ignores useful criticism	Learns from criticism
Threatened by others	Inspired by others

So how can you identify whether your child displays a fixed or growth mindset for their tennis? You have probably got some idea already.

Fixed mindsets

People with fixed mindsets believe that ability is all about talent. If a child has a fixed mindset and believes they are successful because they are talented, they will not strive for more challenging practices or higher-level tournament. If they are winning they may became smug and too comfortable in their ability to succeed. If they think that another child is better than them or beats them, they will consider that their opponent will always be better than them. In addition if they lose a match they think they should win or if they are struggling to develop a skills, their confidence will plummet and they can become very dispirited.

If your child tends towards having a fixed mindset they may say some of the following statements:
- I'll beat him/her because I'm better than them.
- He/She is no good because their rating is…
- I don't need to warm up for this match.
- I always hit my backhand topspin out.
- I'll never be able to hit a kick service.

- I'll never beat him.
- I can't believe he/she beat me because I'm miles better.
- How did I lose that!
- I can't do it.
- I don't want to play them as they always win.
- I'm rubbish!

Growth mindsets

A child who tends towards the growth mindset continuum will believe that they can get constantly better. They will look at players who are beating them and will consider that is the practice they are doing. They will want to complete certain drills so they can improve their skill.

If your child has a growth mindset they may make the some of the following comments:
- I worked really hard in practice today and I'm improving.
- I'd like to play in some higher levels tournaments and have tougher matches.
- I will be able to beat them; I just need to improve my second serve.
- They must have practiced loads to get that good.
- Can I practice…?
- It worked hitting it to their backhand, I'll try that again.
- Can you tell me what I need to improve on?
- Why do you think I lost?
- I can't do it…yet!

Building a growth mindset

Developing a growth a mindset in our children is an aim for many parents. Children with a growth mindset will be more able to cope with setbacks and when things go wrong they are less likely to lose focus. A child with a growth mindset may even find losses motivating and give them a fresh impetus to practice an element of their game. A child with a very strong growth mindset will find success in their learning or their training. So rather than winning a match it is what they have improved on that is the most important driver. (This is a key tenet of 'The inner game of tennis' by Timothy Gallwey, which is well worth reading)

If we know what mindsets are and we can recognise where our children are on the mindset continuum then one of our challenges is to consider what we can do to develop a growth mindset in our child. However it is important before we begin that we must never criticise our child for showing a fixed mindset. If our child has played a match and is displaying fixed mindset language we should only encourage, however hard that may be. If we think about our own lives, one negative comment can often be worth 50 positive ones.

You can ask your child questions to try and help develop their growth mindset:

General Questions	Tennis Questions
What did you today that made you think hard?	What did you practice today that made you think or work hard?
What happened today that made you keep going on?	When you were practising your kick serve what made you keep trying?
What strategy are you going to try now?	When you next practice what do you want to work on?
What will you do to challenge yourself today?	What do you want to practice or work on today?
What will you do to solve this problem?	In this match what are you going to try? What else could you try?

How you talk to and praise your child can help your child move towards either a fixed or a growth mindset. Think about what you are saying and whether unintentionally your comments suggest that your child has permanent traits and you are judging them rather than giving the message that they are developing themselves and you are interested in their development.

When you praise them, try not to praise them for their intelligence or their talent. Its very easy to say when they've done a piece of homework, you're really clever or when they've won a tennis match, you're great player. We want to build their confidence up but actually at the same time we are reinforcing a fixed mindset, that talent and intelligence are predetermined. Instead what we need to try and praise is their strategies, their efforts or their choices.

> *Praise should deal, not with the child's personality attributes, but with his efforts and achievements."*
> *Carol Dweck*

Growth mindset praise could sound like this:
- You worked really hard today.
- I could really see what you've been practicing on in that match.
- I liked it when you got into a long rally and kept going.
- I was impressed that you kept going for your winners.
- I'm really proud of you for trying so hard.
- You deserved to win because of all your practice and how hard you've been working.

1. Does the idea of mindsets resonate with you?

2. Where do you think you child is on the mindset continuum at the moment?

3. What actions could you take to build their growth mindset?

4. How can you use praise to reinforce your child's growth mindset?

The power of yet

The final aspect of developing a growth mindset is making use of the power of 'yet'. If you are really working towards a growth mindset, you are saying that if you keep working you will keep improving. When your child says they cannot do something, try and turn it around with by using the work yet.

Child says	You reply
I can't hit a backhand volley	You're not making your backhand volleys yet.
I've never won a competition.	You've not won a competition yet.
I'll never be able kick serve.	You're not hitting your kick serves yet

Final Word

I hope this chapter has you given you some food for thought and some ideas on how you can develop a growth mindset in your child. If you want to find out more, I would suggest reading 'Mindset: How you can fulfil your potential' by Carol S. Dweck.

Finally I am not saying that mindset is the answers nor is it an easy process to follow but I do believe it is another useful set of ideas for you to use as a parent and a tennis parent.

12 HELPING YOUR CHILD ANALYSE THEIR PERFORMANCE

Hopefully chapter 10 showed that immediately after your child finishes a match is not necessarily the best time to help them analyse their performance. Most children will grade their performance purely according to whether they have won or lost.

> *'I'm a perfectionist. I'm pretty much insatiable. I feel there's so many things, I can improve upon.'*
> *Serena Williams.*

All sports provide a wealth of statistics and tennis perhaps even more than most. It is easy count successful first serves, second serve faults or the type of shots, which result in winners or faults. There are a number tables in this chapter which will give you some strategies which you could use but as a parent you are looking for ways to emphasise positives and not tell your child what they are doing wrong.

This chapter shows you how to highlight what your child did well, and also what you can do about any weaknesses, which you may have observed.

Finding the positives

When your child move from mini red to orange to green and full ball, there become fewer matches in a day, so there may be days when they only win one match or don't win one at all. In addition the tennis scoring systems means that every game could go to deuce but the score in the set could be 6-0 (or 4-0) in a short set. A child could win a short set 4-0 yet the score in points may be 16-12 with sudden death deuces.

In green ball and full ball it is good to encourage your child to look for positives in their performance rather than simply the number of matches that they win. This could be through highlighting rallies or shots, which went really well as discussed in the positive diary in chapter 9. You could also use a more statistical approach to show your child how they are improving. Different methods work with different children.

Many coaches will work with players on how to develop a point. Moving between trading shots i.e. safe shots when the players are returning safely, to building shots, i.e. when the player is probing for a weakness and increasing the pressure before going for the finishing shot. Many junior players will rush to finishing shot with high risk and can quickly lose the point.

In addition if a player is hitting finishing shots very quickly in a rally, their ratio of winning and losing points could be similar but they just do not get into the game as it can become very stop start without any real flow.

In such a circumstance you could watch a match and keep a record of the shots in the rally and whether the point was won or lost. The following diagram shows such a record that could be kept.

The number represents the number of shots in the rally. The little plus or minus shows whether your child lose the point and the asterisk shows whether they miss their first serve or second serve. This diagram does not keep a record of the opponents missed first serve so the asterisk then shows when they have hit double faults. (See the second point in game 3)

Serving	Points	Score
No	- + - + - + - + - - 2 2 2 2 14 2 8 4 2	0 -1
Yes	+ - + + - + 6 * 8 4 2 8 * *	1 – 1
No	- + - + - - 2 * 4 8 4 2	1-2

In this situation the child is 2-1 down in games and each game they lost reached deuce. It is also noticeable that any points lasting more than 6 shots, they have won. You could talk about the difficulty of getting warmed up and into the game with lots of short of points and highlight that this is a high-risk strategy, which on another day may not have proved effective. Finally you would also have a record of the first serves they made and you could compare their double faults to the opponent.

Unforced errors

How many times have you watched your child receive a soft second serve, their eyes light up, they move to attack the ball, unleash a forehand topspin down the line… only for the ball to sail a metre long? Maybe they've hit a good serve, their opponent plays a short return to their backhand, they stalk the ball, hit a vicious double handed backhand only to hit the ball too flat and the ball hammers into the net.

It is heart breaking to see the look of anguish on your child's face and the slump in their body language. You may remind yourself of your child's coach's words that the important thing is that their intention are right, the execution will come with practice.

This may be right but at the same time, we want our children to have success, win matches and there is no doubt that children who can reduce their unforced error count will win more matches. You may be talking to your child about whether they can reduce their number of unforced errors so that they stay in the point longer. Children often comment that other players they don't necessarily hit the ball any harder but they just keep getting it back.

Your own child may be playing against a really good player and they maybe concentrating on staying in the point as long as possible. If you can see they are playing really well why not keep a record so that you give your child evidence on their improvement.

The following grid could be used to keep track of unforced errors in a match and the number of winners, which the players hit.

Game		Unforced Errors	Winners	Match score
Game 1	Player 1	IIII	I	
	Player 2	II		1-0
Game 2	Player 1	III	I	
	Player 2		I	2-0
Game 3	Player 1	IIII	I	
	Player 2	III		3-0

This grid shows that player 1 is losing the set. They have actually hit more winners but their unforced error score is much higher.

Tennis parent story…

This week, coach was unavailable so I took on the role of hitting partner. We agreed that we'd both work on reducing the number of unforced errors we made. First we warmed up and played lots of points but did not keep count. In the second half of our practice we began to play tiebreaks but created our own scoring system. The agreement was, if you won the rally with a winner you got one point but if you lost the rally with an unforced error, the other player got two points. This really focussed our minds. However at the same time we did not just 'moonball' or play 'pattercake' tennis we went for our shots. By the fourth tiebreak he was making fewer unforced errors and hence thrashed me. We both left the court with smiles on our faces.

Are they unforced errors?

You could count unforced errors and winners and it can appear your child is making more unforced errors. However this may not be the true tale. It could be two players slugging it out from all round the court. They could be putting everything into their shots and rally's being regularly longer than 20 shots. Here an unforced error isn't an unforced error. If you've hit 15 shots from all angles of the court and run 100s of metres and then hit it into the net, you haven't made an unforced error, instead you've been pressurised. In terms of the score line your child could have lost comfortably but inside they may come off the court pleased knowing they'd played well and that they had forced the other player to work hard to win the match.

Dealing with 'negatives'

One of the difficult thing as a parent is what to when you can see your child is doing something badly. There are some times when a little intervention can make a big difference, especially in mini-tennis when they have a number of matches in one day.

For instance if it is a very windy day, when the wind is behind them they need to step in, as their opponent's shots will often land short. There may be a technical thing that you can quickly alter such as you notice during serving they are not tossing the ball high enough.

It is very easy to give too much feedback and at the wrong time. For instance your child could come off and once they've calmed down ask why they'd lost. You may have noticed that they were being dragged into the net and then the other child was hitting it past or over them. If you give this feedback in too much detail, you child may concentrate on this but the next opponent may never do this and actually they need to come into the net a little more.

Often the best advice is just to write down the issues you noticed. When you look at them a day later, you may realise that you have written down far too many things and just highlight one or two items. Rather than then discussing them with your child, have a chat with your child's coach or send them email. After all this is why you pay a coach, to work on aspects of your child's game.

Long-term analysis

The long-term aim is that your child begins to analyse their own performance dispassionately and can work out what they need to improve. If they can see what is going wrong in a match and make a change, this is very impressive. This takes an awful long time and a lot of practice. You and your child's coach will need to do a lot of careful modelling and years of patience to get there. The starting point would be your child highlighting something that didn't go too well and then share this with coach to work on in the next session.

'You have to find it. No one else can find it for you'
Bjorn Borg

1. How do you record positive aspects of your child's tennis matches?

2. Do you have your own analysis method?

3. How does your child respond if you try to highlight an area of weakness you have observed?

Final Word

Our role as a tennis parents is to highlight that positivity of progress. Our unforced error would be just looking at the score line or our own statistics. Our winner is any smile on our children's faces.

13 PLANNING YOUR CHILD'S SCHEDULE

It tends to be parents who are booking the tennis lessons and making the competition entries. You may find that this quickly becomes a treadmill of one competition after another as you look for the next good result. If a completion goes badly, you may feel that you to get back on 'the horse' as soon as possible. If your child gets a good result, you can believe you need to surf the positive wave.

 The chapter considers whether your child should take a mid-season break, what a good mix of competition and practice is, and what grades of competitions are most suitable for your child.

Competition Schedule

Many parents feel that the best person to give on-court advice to their child is the tennis coach. Whether you follow this maxim or not, you will still retain ownership of your child's tournament schedule. In the UK, red ball tennis is for under 8s and you will often find children in year 1 and year 2 of primary school playing in competitions. Matches are refereed and are generally quick affairs. Children may get upset when losing a certain match but they quickly bounce back.

'Control the things you can control'
Sam Stosur.

When children move to orange ball either in year 3, if they have played a lot red ball or during the year 4, it is amazing the number of tournaments that some children play. They may be playing competitively both days at the weekend with parents driving them around the country.

You will know your child and whether they thrive on competition. The joy of orange ball is that matches are short and children often get four or five matches (perhaps even more) in an afternoon or a day. The result is that children do not get too exhausted from their matches and hopefully recover speedily from any defeats.

In orange the grading of tournaments will give you an indication of how tough the matches with grade 3 regional tournaments often attracting many stronger players whereas the field for grade 4 and grade 5 local tournaments can be less challenging.

Most children will benefit from playing in a range of tournaments so that they have different chance of achieving success. It seems a shame for a child to only play grade 3 competitions and never get to a final. It would be better for your child to have different experiences. You need to try and provide a balance for your child between lessons and competitions. There is plenty of time for children to play in competitions in their tennis career, they do not need to compete all the time now, as you do run the risk of burning them out.

Green ball tennis provides a much bigger, physical and mental challenge to Orange ball. Physically children are covering the whole court and even with short sets and Fast4, a match can last over ninety minutes. Mentally it is tough too, as player have to relearn how to win matches. Children realise that there are no easy games and that ratings below G1* can be very variable. You could play a Green 4 player who is awesome and you can have an easy win against G1 player.

As matches are longer your child will have fewer of them in a day. A large summer grade 3 tournaments could be an elimination draw and if your child loses their first two matches, they are out. Equally in a one-day competition, your child could play four matches in one day, which can be tiring.

Increasingly in grade 4 and 5 green and full ball tournaments the focus is on 'fast 4' tennis. In green ball this could be one short set up to four games, so players can play more matches

At full ball there is a regular range of grade 2 national tournaments, which have high numbers of ranking points available. These competitions tend to be over three day and are often greatly oversubscribed just to get a place. As a parent you may have it as an aim for your child to play in such an event. Think carefully though, if your child is one of the lowest ranked players in the tournament and will struggle to win a match, is it better keeping them in grade 3 and grade 4 tournaments so they win more matches?

A second option in full ball is playing up an age group. You may find that an U14 grade 5 is similar in standard to an U12 grade 4 and is worth similar ranking points. The same is true of an U14 grade 4 in comparison to a U16 grade 5. I am always hesitant in placing my children in a tournament when I think there is perhaps only one child who I think they have a chance of beating. It is always a long journey home when you have lost all your matches whatever the mileage.

If your child has a couple of bad experiences in a higher-grade tournament, quickly drop them down a level of competition to see if they can win some matches. This becomes even more important at Under 12, and you may decide that even if they played regularly in grade 3s at green ball, now is the time to play in a range of tournaments.

Also consider which venues you and your child like. This could include the type of courts some children have a surface they particularly dislike such as carpet or clay and you may choose to miss those clubs. Some venues are lovely places; you could go to a rural location with great views, to the seaside or a fantastic sports club. There are some tournaments in the summer, which still take place on grass. This might seem a real treat to your child after watching Wimbledon.

So take the opportunity to see different places; you will then enjoy the experience more too. In the summer you could use a grade 3 tournament as an opportunity for a little holiday camping holiday or create a tennis tour by playing a mixture of tournaments over a few days.

Boys and Girls

In mini-tennis, tournament are often mixed and if you have a daughter you may have to think more carefully about competition entry. You can find that a mixed grade 4 tournament is a similar standard to a girl's grade 3. If your older child is a boy you may not have really noticed the difference between the genders just thinking there are some very good boy tennis players and some excellent girl tennis players. You will notice there is a smaller pool of female players. You may not consider whether the boys play in a different style or not from the girls they compete against.

Once you have a daughter, even at red ball you will be aware of the difference. This is first noticeable in outdoor matches with felt red balls when boys try to whack the ball as hard as they can, especially on their serve, whereas the girls try to manoeuvre the ball around the court. The boys seemed to either hit winners or hit it out and the girls barely get into the rally.

As you move into Orange ball, the gap in terms of power and aggression appears to widen with many of the girls playing a different style of game. For this reason, you may look for only girls' only tournament and your daughter may say she prefers them.

Tennis parent story…

The big difference I notice between the way boys and girls play tennis is how they manage their emotions. I was at an orange competition with two eight player draws, one for boys and girls. When the boys were playing, there were constant shouts of anguish as points were won and lost. Once the boys moved from the groups to the compass draw, for seemingly every match there were tears and heartache from the losers.

Yet the girls competition was played in almost an eerie silence with the only sounds that of the scores and the whack of racket on ball or thud of ball against the court. I did not see one tear shed by any of the girls; from the girl who lost a hard fought final to the girl who lost all her matches.

This was amplified at a grade 2 orange tournament. The girls got on and played their matches. Whereas in every single boys match the referee was called onto court as they argued whether the ball was in or out. The boys got so upset after they lost a match, that it really made me question whether there should be national tournaments at this young age as the boys did not seem able to cope. I was relieved to see that the LTA decided to stop orange national tournaments.

The mid-season break

Do you ever wonder if your child has been sucked into a constant round of one competition after another? Then ask yourself, is this healthy? Finally consider, how will this impact on your child's long-term love of the game?

You can quickly find by the time that your child reaches the age of 11, they can have been playing pretty much none-stop for the last three years. First it was red ball and the race to get the Red 1 rating as well as chasing medals. Secondly the move to Orange ball with the challenge to get from Orange 4 to Orange 1, with a final push in the summer of getting those 20 wins and the holy grail of the Orange 1*. Competition then changes to Green ball and whether it would be possible to get the Green 1* by playing enough G1 and G1* players in Grade 3 competitions whilst still play enough grade 4s and 5s to give more chance of winning some tournaments.

Yellow ball then provides a new list of collectibles with the addition of county, regional and national rankings to ratings. If your child has an early growth spurt you may find their body begins to creak.

If you think of the comparison to other sportsmen and women, they have some kind of break. There has been a debate over a number of years about a mid-season break in the football season and that is in addition to the summer break. It has often been commented that after a World Cup summer footballers struggle the following season.

In tennis, players will generally have a break from competition in November and December. There has also been discussion over should this window be longer prior to the Australian Open. I can remember John McEnroe being insistent that Andy Murray should take a break and Roger Federer often takes breaks before the grass court season.

It is important to remember that young athletes are constantly growing which places considerable stress on their joints and muscles. Hence they are at more risk of injury than adults. Finally, does the constant round of tournament-to-tournament run the risk of taking the fun out of the game?

Why not plan specific breaks from competition over the next year and consider when is the best time to place these? You could follow the pros and place one window from October half term to Christmas holidays and then maybe have another break after Easter before AEGON Club tennis starts? You may decide to have a break during the spring term or perhaps during your own summer holiday.

Try and avoid the 'knockout'

Do you ever wonder why children stop competing in tennis? You might look around at tournament fields in the second year of under 12's or in under 14s and think where are the children who used to enter competitions. You might be the parent of a younger child who is being asked to play up in AEGON under 12s or 14s and again wonder the older players are?

There are many reasons why children stop competing; different children will have stopped for a range of reasons. I think one reasons is that children lose their resilience and fall out of love with competition from having played too many tight matches.

Sports commentators will talk about boxers and the number of hard fights they have had. Knockouts and knockdowns greatly age fighters, as do the number of battles when they have fought toe to toe for twelve founds. This means fighters like Wladimir Klitschko can fight into there 40s, whereas other retire much earlier.

In the world of junior tennis, I believe we have to try and guard our children from too many tight losses. These are the equivalent of the toe-to-toe slugfests. I think the match a child loses 4-0, 4-1 does not have a massive impact on them. Instead those two-hour matches with the results like 5-4,3-5, 12-10 are the ones that really affect a child and too many, can make them not want to compete.

Some coaches and parents consider that such tight losses do not affect children in their early teens and that these battles will increase their resilience. It is only when they reach their mid teens this management become important. I believe that every child is different.

So if your child is the type of player who has lots of tight matches, perhaps the advice is not to play as many competitions as the child who either wins or loses easily does. It is not the number of matches they play instead it is the number of wars they have, which have the long-term impact on a child.

1. How many competitions has your child played in comparison to their peers?

2. Do you feel you are in car travelling to tournament every weekend?

3. Can you schedule a break from competitions for your child and when would this best fit?

4. Have you a list of competitions and lovely venues, which you think will help inspire your child?

Final Word

'I love the winning, I can take losing but most of all I love to play'
Boris Becker

For many parents the aim of the tennis journey is that our children gain a skill, which they enjoy using in their teenage years and through adulthood. Not that they are burnt out and jaded before they turn thirteen. Therefore you need to think carefully about how many competitions to enter and when to take a break. It is much better for your child to be asking you to play more rather than not wanting to get in the car for another tournament.

14 TENNIS AND SCHOOL

As the hours of training and the number of competitions increase, the balance between school and tennis can become more challenging. When children are in primary school they often seem to have more mental and physical energy than when they move into secondary school and adolescence kicks in.

All sports parents have to think carefully about how they manage their children's training with their school life. As children get older, particularly choices of school could be required with their associated costs.

'My father actually moved out from Chicago just so he could play tennis 365 days a year, so it was - it was a place we played every day. We played before school. We played after school. We woke up. We played tennis. We brushed our teeth in that order.'
Andre Agassi

This chapter aims to give you some ideas and questions about how you can make the most of primary school, choose the right secondary school and manage the transition from primary to secondary school. If you child does play at a very high level in their teenage years, then there will be more specialist choices for post 16 education and higher education which this chapter will touch upon.

Primary School

It is unlikely that your child will been introduced to tennis through school but instead it will probably have been via a local club. There are very few state primary schools where tennis is played as an organised school sport. In fact it would be very rare to find a state primary with a tennis court. In the independent sector, some schools may play tennis matches but the summer term is very short and is often dominated by the main team sports and athletics.

I felt sad because everyday I had to wake up early to practice before going to school. After school I had to go back to tennis again, and then after tennis I had homework. I didn't have time to play.
Li Na

The result is that few primary schools or teachers will understand your child's tennis. They will imagine it is a knock about, with the children barely being able to hit a ball. Perhaps they will find out about your child's pursuit through 'show and tell' if your child wins a sponge or orange ball trophy and takes it into school. Often schools ask children to give presentations on their hobbies using a power point. If you take a short video of your child you can include this in the PowerPoint to give the teacher some idea of what your child is doing. The one thing that you will be asked regularly is 'when we will see them at Wimbledon?'

One of the challenges particularly in green ball is how to fit the hours of practice in, particularly during the winter months. It is often difficult to get indoor court time and coupled with this 9-11 year olds should not be practicing for too long in a single session. They also need their sleep so practicing after 8pm is often not a good idea.

A solution to this is to ask the primary school if your child can come out of school one or two afternoons a week to train. Many primary schools at this age will be focussed upon working towards Maths and English for the child's Key Stage 2 SATs tests and this tends to be concentrated upon in the morning sessions. So a school may be flexible about your child playing tennis some afternoons.

Playing tennis in the afternoon slot can be effective for lots of reasons. Firstly your child is likely to have more energy and concentration at this time rather than after they have completed a day at school. Indoor courts are far less busy so you can easily book them. Lots of coaches do not have much work in this time so you may be able to negotiate a reduced rate with them. Some counties even run performance squads in these slots.

One likely hindrance to this is if a school has a focus on attendance particularly if OFSTED has highlighted this as an area of weakness. They may be reluctant for attendance reasons for your child to be out of school. The target for primary school attendance is currently 96%. So if your child has one afternoon off a week, their attendance will be a maximum of 90% and if they have two afternoons off a week this falls to 80%. In a small school your child's attendance can greatly impact the overall statistics.

There are two ways that you could suggest to the school, which will help them get round this. The first is ensuring your child is still at school when they take afternoon registration. This is often immediately after lunch ends perhaps at 1pm. If you collected your child from school after this time, they have their afternoon register mark. Hence for your school's attendance figures your child is actually classed as present. The second method is to ask the school to code the absence as approved sporting activity (P) as this means for the school's statistics your child is classed as present.

You may on occasion choose to take your child out of school to play in certain competitions. In lots of areas, counties can have very different holidays and you can find that your October half term is different to another and as a result a really good competition is in your child's school term. If you live in the North of the country there are some good competitions in Scotland which are worth looking at if you are prepared to take your child out of school. The same is true as the end of the summer term approaches and you may find that it is worth taking them out of school to play in a prestigious grade 3 tournament.

Unfortunately many school are less forgiving about the Wimbledon fortnight. If you are lucky enough to be allocated tickets in the ballot, often schools will not accept this as a reason for absence. Hence taking your child can result in an unauthorised absence. These one-offs are unlikely to have any impact on you or your child.

Secondary Schools

When your child moves to secondary school you may have to think carefully about how you wish to balance tennis and school. In effect you are likely to have four choices.

> *'I chose to stay with tennis and they didn't understand that at school.'*
> *John Newcombe*

The first is a normal secondary school, which your child attends for every session and you try and fit in training after school and at the weekend. This is not always easy especially when they are balancing homework and other school activities. The result is that your child may not be able to fit in the hours that some other children do in those first few years of secondary school. The advantage of this is that your child is enjoying the full range of school activities. Your child will make a wide range of friends and have different pastimes. It is hoped that such an approach will reduce burn out but you may find that your child initially plateaus in comparison to those children playing at a high level with a different style of schooling.

The second is a normal secondary school but you make an agreement with the school that they will miss some sessions from school so that can train at a local club. Your child will be able to fit in more training as a result and possibly at a lower price because as we discussed earlier, coaches and courts are less busy. There are some difficulties with this option. Firstly other children will see your child as different because they are not following the normal timetable. Your child will miss certain lessons, which they will then have to catch up on. If it is a practical subject, this is something that they will not be able to simply copy up so are missing part of school. Your child may feel that just by being out of school two afternoons a week, they are missing out on things and feel left out.

A third option is to choose a school, which has a tennis specialism. There are state and independent schools, which have links with the LTA and offer this opportunity. There are not many of these schools in the country so you would be lucky if there is one near where you live. This can be an expensive option, as you will have to pay boarding fees. There are very different views on child boarding and you will have your own thoughts on whether you would like to do this. Some schools will have bursaries and scholarships, which you can access to help pay for the fees.

A fourth option is to look at a tennis performance centres, which also offers education. This is likely to provide the best tennis as the whole day will be based around training and your child will be with other children who are totally committed to tennis. The education on offer is likely to be more limited perhaps only covering Maths, English, Science and PE. Again there might not be a venue near where you live so this could involve boarding or lodging with a local family. Such a centre can be very intense and not all children find this an easy atmosphere to work in.

There is a fifth option but this is very rare. Any parent can decide to home school their child and they have responsibility for ensuring that the child is following a suitable education. Very few local authorities make any checks on parents who are following this route. This can be popular for coaches who are training their own children as they can work with them in the daytime and then still coach and run club sessions at evenings and weekends to bring in an income.

The best advice is to discuss this carefully with your child and coach to see what they think. It is interesting that many children who do choose the specialist routes often return to normal schooling either because of frequent injuries or because they have fallen out of love with the game and they just want a 'normal schooling'. Many neutrals observers may suggest trying to keep education as normal as possible and then as the child gets older allow them to choose if they wish to drop certain subjects to train more.

1. What is your view on the balance between education and tennis?

2. Speak to other parents about the choices that they have made for their children's tennis.

3. Talk to your child about they what they would really like to do?

Transition from Primary to Secondary School

The new school year brings challenges to all children and their families. This can be increased for children who are juggling the pressure and commitment of playing competitive tennis. This can be even greater for children who are starting a new school and a new phase of education.

For the vast majority of children in this country, the big change to secondary education is at the age of 11. (I recognise that some parts of the country have middle schools and also in the Independent sector this may be at 13 or 14).

It is easy to underestimate the huge change of moving from a primary school to secondary school and hence the impact this may have on your child. At the same time your child is in the second year of under 12s tennis and you may be thinking this is the time to plot a rise up the national ranking as they are now one of the older ones in this age bracket. You may already be planning a campaign of tournaments through till Christmas alongside an increase in practice and coaching court time. Hoping to maximise your child's increased strength.

However just pause for a minute and think about the challenge your child is facing at their new school.

They've gone from an environment were they knew everybody and had a very established social group and now they have to make new friends. They could be in in a form group were they know no-one and then may move to different groups with a new set of pupils. For anyone this is very nerve wracking and tiring.

At primary school they will have likely to have been in one class with one teacher. They now are moving classroom at least five times, walking across a school, carrying a heavy bag. They may have to get up earlier in the day and be on their feet walking to school or waiting at a bus stop. It is surprising how physically tiring this.

They could have fifteen different subjects with as many different teachers. Each will be pushing the children mentally. On top of this is the homework at the end of day which now can take 90minutes an evening, when at primary school this may have been 90minutes a week.

Finally your child could be having a rapid growth spurt with a cocktail of hormones running through them.

Is this the time to be upping your child's tennis or perhaps this may be the time to just focus on the core of their tennis programme up till half term. You may actually reduce the duration of practice a little in comparison to before the summer and you may put a pause on tournaments.

Perhaps this autumn term is not the time to be pushing. Even when you have got to half term, children still have to cope with the dark of November and December before the Christmas holidays. I can remember as a secondary school headteacher seeing the year 7 children looking exhausted in school assemblies prior to Christmas, thinking they just needed the break.

It is mentally exhausting playing competitions and your child needs considerable resilience and reserves of energy to give their best. They may struggle with this as they to move into secondary school.

Remember there is always time to play more competitions or do more lessons when your child is ready. What you can't get back as easily is if your child starts to fall out of love with tennis because of the pressure they will feel during this term.

Tennis parent story…

When my son moved to secondary school I did not make enough allowances for the challenge that secondary school would bring. In year 6 he had taken one afternoon off school a week to work with his coach, which he loved, as well as evening and weekend training and competing regularly.

As with most boys, year 7 was very tiring and life was becoming a military operation to fit in homework and training. Playing competitions became another source of stress added to that of secondary school. I did not get the balance right and he started to fall out of love with the sport.

With my daughter I have followed a very different route in the first term of secondary school. Training has been reduced so that she can have time to fit in homework and has more energy for other extra-curricular activities. She has played in very few competitions and only in the holidays. Yes she has slipped down the rankings list and her rating will not increase as quickly as it could have done but this is a long-term investment in the hope that she will continue to enjoy her tennis.

Post 16

Young people have so many choice around post 16 education, so that if your child is still competing regularly at this age, you can find some really interesting options. There are all the options from when considering secondary school. In addition a number of post 16 colleges offer tennis based programmes were your child can train, take their coaching certificates and study a PE based qualification. Some sixth forms will offer similar provision too. A standard post 16 environment, school or college will be likely to offer flexibility so your child can complete the training that they want to.

Then in higher education there are probably a seemingly infinite number of choices including obtaining a tennis scholarship to an American College or University. Talk to coaches about routes other young people have taken and see if any inspire your child.

Final Word

Many children do balance their tennis and school and make good progress with both. They key is to look at your child and consider what is best for them. Try not to compare them with other children and apply their schedule and choices on your child as this may not work. Even comparing siblings may not work.

You also have to accept that flexibility is important. What is right for your child in year 7 may not be in year 8. You must also think about your child's future and I would argue that receiving a well-rounded education with a good set of grades could give your child so many other options in the future. I have always believed that as parents and educators we should be trying to keep as many doors open for our children for as long as possible.

15 STOPPING PLAYING

One of the most traumatic things for tennis parents and their children is if the child makes the decision that they no longer wish to play. So much money and emotions will have been invested, that parents can feel let down and children feel extremely guilty. In this chapter we will examine the further benefits of tennis and what is life after tennis for you and your child?

> *'There were many occasions in my career where I could have given up, where I asked myself whether I would ever make it'*
> *Amelie Mauresmo.*

Levels of 'quitting'

Hearing the word quit can provoke strong emotions but as parents we have to consider that there are many different levels of playing tennis. Your child may no longer wish to play in a competition every weekend or train over ten hours week but that does not stop them from being a tennis player. Many adults gain a lot of pleasure from playing social tennis once or twice a week. We need to consider that all skills our children have learnt from tennis will stay with them for a life and the more we force them to do something, the more we push them away

What are the early warning signs?

If you can spot early warning signs of your child wanting to give up, then you have an opportunity to adjust your child's diet of tennis, and stop your child's view hardening, that they want to give up. You need to look for the following:

- Does your child complain when you try and get them ready for a competition?
- Has your child ever faked an injury?
- Is she resistant to practicing on her own, or does she complain constantly when she's reminded to practice?
- Can you get through a discussion about tennis without it leading to whining or some kind of conflict?
- Does the activity seem to build your child's self-confidence -- or does it tear it down?
- Does your child appear to give up during tournaments?
- Does your child regularly say, ' I hate tennis?'

What can you do?

At this stage there are interventions that you can make which could mean that this is a passing phase. Talk to your child about which elements of tennis they find fun and enjoy? It might be there are certain squads or children that they enjoy playing with. Look to give your child as many of these opportunities as possible.

Many children go through a stage were they find competing too stressful and become very upset and angry by the process. If this is the case for your child, by continuing to enter them in competitions you will push them away from the sport. It really does not matter what their ranking or rating is.

It is common for parent to ask their child if they want to play in a competition, they say yes but when you get to the day of the competition or the day before, they rebel and refuse to play. In reality this is their way of saying they do not want to compete but only realise this when faced with a competition. The best advice; is to give your child a break from competing but see if they will stick with some of their practice sessions. Though you may reduce this too. You may find over time that they drift back into competition through team tennis or doubles. If they do, be very careful to watch the warning signs in future of your child competing too much again.

You may find the reverse is true, in that they have a spell when they do not want to practice but actually love competing. This is less common but you need to be aware of this possibility. Again, reduce the practice sessions and allow them to compete.

The important thing is to look for what they like doing and use this to help rekindle their enthusiasm. There has been a growth in alternative tennis activities whether it is paddleball, beach tennis or touch tennis. Your child may enjoy the fun of trying one of these.

Tennis parent story…

The first time my child said, they hated tennis, it really hurt. You hear your child say it at tournaments but presume they mean that they hate losing. But if losing becomes too frequent with the accompanying emotional rollercoaster, this negativity can cross over to everything tennis. I knew all that but it still made me so cross that I wanted to take away all his trophies. As after all if they hate tennis how could they want those tokens of the game around them? After listening for a few weeks what they really meant is that tennis was no longer fun.

We stopped squad practices and lessons for a while. I looked for anything about tennis that seemed fun and one rainy Saturday we hit on the idea of playing touch tennis (sponge ball tennis). That was fun tennis in their eyes and it got him on court and to the tennis club. We had a great time, even though he insisted on telling me he hated tennis! What I focused on was finding some opportunities for him to play low-key fun tennis.

It seems to have worked as he is now back on court. I do not know if we'll ever go back to the competition circuit but if he plays some squad sessions a couple of times a week, he is staying fit and keeping his skill going which he will always have.

What about doubles?

When your child first started playing tennis it was fun. All those little games in mini tennis squads when the children were running around laughing. It wasn't who was hitting the ball best, it was just children playing.

When we look at adult tennis from professional to a club afternoon, it's doubles that provides most the fun. There are the crazy rallies that occur to just having company on court next to you, somebody to talk too. Certainly when Jamie Murray won the mixed doubles title at Wimbledon with Jelena Jankovic in 2007, it looked like they were having fun on court together. Children benefit from that just as much as adults do, probably more so.

If you child says tennis is no longer fun, could you encourage doubles in their play? What about:

- Your child reducing their individual lessons and having some doubles lessons in a group. This should be far less intense and pressured but still good practice.
- Take your child to adult social tennis and see if they can join in the club doubles, so they get the opportunity to see fun tennis being played (hopefully!)
- AEGON tennis allows children to play some doubles matches
- Enter a doubles competition.
- What ever it is, see if it can put a smile on their tennis playing face!

Being a hitting buddy

Your child will have built up a lot of skills along the way and can play tennis at a good standard. They will have had countless hours of training and worked with lots of coaches. Competitions will also have thrown so much at them, which they have dealt.

Your child may be able to use all this experience to hit with some younger children at the club. Being in this position of authority may really motivate your child. They may also be able to earn a little bit of money from the process too. Whilst your child may no longer which to compete, they may find that coaching offers an opportunity for them to use the skills they have developed over the years.

They still want to quit

There can come a moment when your child looks at you and says they want to quit and you realise that they really do mean it and nothing that you say will make any difference.

'Tennis is just a game, family is forever.'
Serena Williams

However upset you are, shocked or incredulous, remember you are the adult. The best thing that you can do is just to try and keep your mouth closed. It would be too easy to speak from your emotions, to think about all the time and money that you have invested and feel that they are just throwing away. Whatever you say in this state will be hurtful and you must not say it.

Instead you have to try and see it from your child's perspective. The chances are they have wrestled with this moment too. Tennis for our children can be part of their identity and it has been something that has taken up so many hours of their lives. They will also know how upset you will be and it will have been so hard for them to tell you.

You need to try and get them to explain why they want to quit. However this may not be right moment and instead you could suggest having a chat about it later and think about questions you could ask them:
- Why do they want to quit?
- Are they unhappy playing?
- Do they have a problem with their coach?
- Or is it an issue with another teammate? Is
- Are they burnt out and simply need a rest from the sport?
- Is there a different sport they would like to play?

You must listen carefully to their reasons and their feelings. You need to put aside your needs and feelings about their continuance in tennis and what you think they can achieve. Their sport is NOT about you, it is about them! Depending upon their responses, you then need to help them make a decision that is best for them.

Just because your child wishes to quit tennis, it does not mean they are starting an unhealthy precedent that they will give up on another things when the going gets tough. You have to think about how much they have achieved and how much they have put in. They are not quitting when the going gets difficult, they have already come through lots of challenge and difficulties on court.

In fact quitting may be the right choice for your child's health particularly if your child is struggling to meet the challenges of tennis. There has been some Canadian research that discovered that, people who can disengage from unattainable goals enjoy better well-being and experience fewer symptoms of everyday illness than do people who have difficulty disengaging from unattainable goals.

If you allow your child to disengage from tennis with good grace and keep the door open with the club, who knows what they may choose to do in the future. There are many children who have taken a rest from competitive tennis in their teens and then picked up a racket again at university and got back into the sport.

1. How would you feel if your child decided they no longer wished to play tennis?

2. What activities can you encourage your child to do so that they have other things in their lives?

3. What do you think your child has learnt from tennis that they can apply in other aspects of their lives?

Final Word

Your child quitting tennis may be one of the toughest moments of your parenthood and it may be a trauma that goes on for many months as you both try to fill the void that is left without all the practice and competitions. You have to focus on all the things they have learnt, all the experiences that they have had. Try and remember it is not about tennis, it is what your child has learnt along the way.

16 LOOKING AFTER YOURSELF

If you look around any tennis court during a competition it is easy to recognise who are the parents. You have probably stood there playing every shot, jerking when a ball is hit into the net. Sharing every tear and yearning to see your child happy. Many tennis parents put the needs of their children first and forget about themselves. Being a parent can be stressful and tennis can certainly add to this. You will be able to cope with this far better if you take care to look after yourself.

This chapter will give you some tips as how you can manage your own physical and mental fitness alongside your tennis parenting.

'A smile is a curve which can straighten out a lot of problems'

Being court side - Training

If every hour your child plays tennis, you are sitting by the side of the court this can quickly amount to a huge number of hours over the course of a week. It is natural that when your child is playing in tournament you will to watch those matches but do you really need to watch every shot of practice?

If you are lucky enough that your child's tennis training is at a health club, try to use those facilities. After a busy day at work or looking after the children, 7pm may not be the ideal time for a want to do a gym work but if there is a pool, sauna or steam room, this is a great opportunity to try and chill for half an hour.

If it is the daytime, then try and do some exercise yourself, whatever is right for you? Maybe this is the time to have that gym induction and receive a personalised programme.

If those facilities do not exist why not force yourself to start jogging? If you have never run before there are lots of programmes to get started. I regularly go running with a fellow tennis dad and as result I have run far further than I ever expected too. If you just feel this is beyond though, go for a walk. If you decide exercise is not for you and you are going to read, work on your laptop or catch up on phone calls, then try and position yourself so that you cannot see the court.

The important thing is not to be stood right next to the court; both your child and their coach need some space to work in. You also need a break from watching every shot that is being hit.

Being court side – Match day

As a tennis parent, I do not think you ever become immune to seeing the feeling of disappointment or anguish in your child when they lose a match. Some parents choose (or are told) not to watch their child play. For those of us who do watch our children we constantly study the ebbs and flows of fortune wondering if this will be a day for smile or tears.

On many occasions we just do not know how the match will end. There will be days when our child loses and we just cannot explain how it happened except for some apparent mystical reason the other child got match point and won it. At other times our own child hits some freak rollercoaster of momentum and wins a match we never expected. Then there is a strange sensation when you just know, that whatever the score, however much your child falls behind, you are certain they will win.

On such days it makes you wonder is it your child's manner that makes you so calm, relaxed or unworried? Or does your confidence transmit itself to them and as a result they never got stressed or anguished.

Statistics are often given on how much communication is due to visual clues. So when we are watching our children ever if we try desperately not to show our concerns, I wonder how much they can pick up on it? What impact does this have on their game and their mental strength? How much can we disguise our feelings and show them we have confidence in them? We are the adult so if we expect our children to behave calmly and keep their emotions in check, whatever fate befalls. Then shouldn't we do the same however much we may wish to react?

So if we are watching our children compete, this is the type of behaviour we should be trying to model:

1) Stay calm… Do you? Are you modelling calm during a match or are you striding about, walking off during key points, making gesticulations or even voicing comments. We may say that it is harder to watch but we are the adults so we need to show the calmness we wish from our child. So chew that gum, sit on your hands, make some notes and breath in slowly and exhale with a smile.

2) Be generous… I am very proud when my son congratulates his opponent when they hit a good shot. We should also do the same, no matter how frustrated we feel. However take care that such comments do not appear as sarcasm towards your child. Applaud the winners from both children.

3) Be friendly… No matter how you feel, congratulate your child's opponent if they won and pass some pleasantries with their parents. You may even be able to socialise with your opponents with your child's opponent during the match. This sets a powerful example to your child that it is only a game.

4) Never ever criticise line calls… However bad it looks, we have to give the opponent the benefit of the doubt. I have tried the

experiment with tennis parents who are my friends, we've watched the same ball and both been equally sure of an opposite line call.

5) Do not make your child the star… No matter how good your child is and how much better they are than their opponent, take time to talk to and even encourage the other children. There is nothing worse than the parent who thinks talking to a weaker child (or the child's parent) is beneath them. Such actions can only breed arrogance when we know the true champions show humility.

6) Be positive… Do not criticise other players, parents, coaches or competition organisers in front of your children. Instead try and show a positive outlook to your child, highlight the good you see not the bad.

7) Finally, remember the 'growth mind-set model' and praise the effort and not the result. The time to really tell your child how great they are and give them a hug is after the terrible, gut wrenching loss.

As I often think, our children are 'mini-me's'; we need to show them how we would truly like them to be.

We have to remember that one of the beauties of tennis is the skill our children build for the rest of their lives yet here is an opportunity for us to learn too. If we can always show our confidence in our children think how useful this could be. Think of those future events; the morning of an examination, the afternoon of their driving test or on the day of a job interview when they need our confidence so they can perform to their full potential.

Perhaps in readiness for those days, it is worth practicing the following maxim: inhale gently… exhale with a smile!

Are you having a bad week?

Have you ever wondered what tennis are you actually watching when you watch your child play? Are you watching what is really happening or what you believe is happening?

We are all used to hearing conversations between a parent and a child after they have lost a match, which begin with the player saying, 'I was miles better than them'. You may have been watching the match as a neutral and be puzzled as through your un-emotional eyes, you felt the better player won. It may have even been your child who was victor and you can have more than a tinge of annoyance as you could feel that your own child's performance has been denigrated. Or you could have been the losing player's parents and you may have watched the match and just be completely confused as to why your child has lost, when you honestly thought they were the better player.

In some ways whilst this may be a delusion, at least it is a positive way of viewing the world and if you are agreeing with your child, you are building their positivity, self-esteem and confidence. It may be that you disagree with your child but go along with conversation because you wish to reduce their pain and hurt.

There are also times when we do not take that positive view of the world when watching our child's matches. You may even do this because of your own mental attitude when you were watching.

Tennis parent story…

I was watching my son take part in a training session with children from other clubs. The session was two hours long and after a stressful week at work, I decided to take the opportunity for some of my own fitness work and went running with the aim of watching the second hour of the session.

After an hour I took my position at a window and began to watch. They were playing tiebreaks to 7. The first tiebreak my son hit lots of double faults and lost to a boy with a similar rating; 7-2. He then played a really good player and lost 7-5 before playing a third playing whom he usually beats and lost 7-1. During those three tiebreaks, I saw all the things wrong that my son was doing and I became increasingly frustrated, a feeling that I retained during that hour.

I was a little cross when my son emerged from the training session but we all know that we shouldn't share those negative thoughts with our children after all it's their game! He didn't want to talk about the training session as he had other things on his mind. It was only later in the evening that he wanted to tell me about the session. I was amazed when he began to tell me, that he had thought he'd played fantastically and proceeded to reel off the scores of four other match tie breaks from the first hour. In hindsight a really strong set of results. I had truly made my decision on how well he'd played more due to the mental state that I was in and a short snapshot of the session. I had watched his performance through my own frustration.

So how do you view the tennis your child is playing? Do we really see the game as it is? Or more likely if we are in good mood are we more positive about what we see? Yet equally and perhaps more worryingly if our week has gone badly do we see a worst performance from our child than actually occurred? Perhaps as spectators we need to work on our own mind-set so that we see the tennis from a balanced perspective.

The curse of the draw

One thing we need to guard against is an addiction to searching competitions, looking at other player's results and studying the draw. It is easy to start spending hours on the LTA website reading such things. You can quickly start looking at competitions entry list and day by day imagine the draw and how well you think your child will do. Then at the last minute players enter or withdraw, there are children there on the day that were not on the list or you get frustrated about the 'fairness' of the draw.

This isn't healthy and is not a good use of time. In addition without realising you can be heaping extra pressure on your child. A common reason from children for not liking tennis is they say their parents are too involved in the process.

Have you tried Mindfulness?

Mindfulness has been one of those words that has been difficult to escape from in recent years, whether it is adult colouring books or in my sphere of education, the introduction of mindfulness into the curriculum for year 7 children.

Have you ever stopped to consider what does Mindfulness actually mean?

There are two definitions given to the noun, mindfulness:
1. The quality or state of being conscious or aware of something, "their mindfulness of the wider cinematic tradition"
2. A mental state achieved by focusing one's awareness on the present moment, while calmly acknowledging and accepting one's feelings, thoughts, and bodily sensations, used as a therapeutic technique.

The way I like to think about mindfulness is bringing my whole attention to the current situation. So if I'm having a conversation with somebody, I'm entirely focussed on that conversation, rather than thinking about the next thing I have to do or the next person I have to speak to. If I am watching a television programme, I'm not checking my twitter feed or some other function on my smart phone instead I am concentrating on the plot or programme content.

I would suggest that mindfulness is interesting to practice during a tennis tournament your child is playing in but only if your child is happy with that. I am not suggesting that you stop choosing to read a newspaper, a book or complete another task during tournament if that keeps you calm or because your child doesn't want you to become to involved in their matches.

What I mean is that if you are both happy with you being fully focussed on your child's play, the mindfulness you should practice is staying in that moment. How often do you sit during a match and begin to work out who your child's next opponent could be? Check your child's results against that player? Or start counting the ranking points or ranking wins your child might gain before they've even completed their first match.

It is often found that by having so many different things in our minds or trying to consider too many different outcomes, what we are inevitably doing is creating additional stress for ourselves. By practicing mindfulness and trying to focus on a smaller number of events, our personal stress should reduce too.

Mindfulness means that as a tennis parent you take one match at a time. Just watch that one game and try to enjoy the skills that your child is displaying? Admire the new shot or serve that they have been working on in practice? Or listen to them encouraging themselves?

You will find that if you can do this, you will be less affected if the tournament does not go according to plan and most importantly be better able as a parent to support your child in their disappointments too.

6 ideas for staying calm

One way of looking after yourself is whether you can keep your emotions in check and stay relaxed so it is not obvious whether your child is winning or losing? Though in fact the real challenge is trying to remain calm. This is the best support you can give your child during a match and then immediately afterwards. Here are six techniques that I have tried in the search for inner calm or other parents have suggested to me.

1. Smile! Yes it sounds simple yet also so hard but it is true that if you can smile you will stay calmer. I particularly like the idea of breathing to calm down and then breathe out with a smile.

2. Make two lists. The first list is all the things that your child has done right. It could be individual shots or rallies and certain points in the match or it could be tactics or strategies that they have employed. The second list is things that have frustrated you during the match. It could be when your child has struggled with their tactics or it could be the way that they have managed their emotions. Before the match ends, pick up the negative list, rip it up and throw the bits in the bin. There is nothing to be gained by sharing these with your child and the act of destroying the list is a way of emptying your mind of them. The positive list is things to

share with your child and you choose when is the most appropriate time.

3. Do some counting! Why not count different aspects of your child's tennis. I have found that by doing this, you reduce your stress over points in the match. You could count how many shots each point lasts or much more complex things too such as those suggested in chapter 12.

4. Try and sit where you do not have an exact view of lines. Do not sit immediately behind the courts or on the baseline. If you have a view akin to that of a line judge you will inevitably see mistakes from both players, many of which are likely to be purely accidental. You will actually have a better view than players who are also trying to hit their shots at the same time. If you sit a little distance from the court you can try and enjoy watching their rallies and at times being unaware of the exact score can be a good feeling.

5. I always have a flask of coffee with me and pour myself lots of small drinks. I never fill my cup as I find the act of taking the top of the flask, pouring a small slug of coffee, putting the lid back on and then sipping the drink quite therapeutic. It is also a small physical activity to do with my hands.

6. Try and practice mindfulness, so stay in the moment rather than trying to work out the rest of the draw and the possible result of each win and loss.

1. What can you do to look after yourself when your child is playing tennis?

2. What exercise could you do during your child's lessons?

3. What makes your calmer and relaxed during competitions?

Final Word

Being a tennis parent can be tough. Many parents find that their children especially when they are younger bounce back from defeats far quicker than they do. We can never do anything about the game that is being played. What we can do is support our children to do the right thing and set them a good example. One way of doing this is to look after our selves.

ABOUT THE AUTHOR

Paul Ainsworth is a former secondary school Head, the author of seven books, a TEDx speaker and regular presenter at national school conferences who now advises school leaders in one of the countries largest group of schools. Most importantly he is the dad of two junior tennis players and in 'Trophies, tears and line calls, he shares his research, practical experience and even his own mistakes so you can make the right choices for your child.

26730615R00076

Printed in Great Britain
by Amazon